INTRODUCING

WOMANIST
THEOLOGY

INTRODUCING

WOMANIST THEOLOGY

Stephanie Y. Mitchem

ORBIS BOOKS

Maryknoll, New York 10545

Fourth Printing, March 2006

Founded in 1970, Orbis Books endeavors to publish works that enlighten the mind, nourish the spirit, and challenge the conscience. The publishing arm of the Maryknoll Fathers and Brothers, Orbis seeks to explore the global dimensions of the Christian faith and mission, to invite dialogue with diverse cultures and religious traditions, and to serve the cause of reconciliation and peace. The books published reflect the views of their authors and do not represent the official position of the Maryknoll Society. To learn more about Maryknoll and Orbis Books, please visit our website at www.maryknoll.org.

Queries regarding rights and permissions should be addressed to:
Orbis Books, P.O. Box 308, Maryknoll, NY 10545-0308.

Published by Orbis Books, Maryknoll, NY 10545-0308

Manufactured in the United States of America

Library of Congress Cataloging-in-Publication Data

Mitchem, Stephanie Y., 1950-
    Introducing womanist theology / Stephanie Y. Mitchem.
      p. cm.
    Includes bibliographical references and index.
    ISBN 1-57075-421-7 (pbk.)
    1. Womanist theology. 2. African American women – Religious life.
I. Title.
BT83.9 .M58 2002
230'.082 – dc21

                                  2002001921

Contents

Preface ix

Acknowledgments xii

PART I

1. Black Women: Race, Gender, and Class 3
   Dynamics of Gender: "Be a Lady"   5
   Dynamics of Race: "But You Are Black"   12
   Questions of Class   15
   Race with Gender with Class: Connecting the Dots   19
   Becoming Womanists   22
   Discussion Questions   24

2. Constructing Theologies 25
   Contours of Theology   26
   Dynamics of Theology   30
   Defining Theology   35
   Defining Liberation Theologies   38
   Culture and Theology   42
   Discussion Questions   45

3. Womanist Theology 46
   "Ordinary" Theologies   46
   Communal Dimensions   49

Constructing Womanist Theology   55

Defining Womanist Theology   60

Discussion Questions   64

PART II

4. **Womanist Constructions** 67

   Signal Texts   68

   Distinctive Approaches   74

   Developing Methods of Womanist Work   77

   Continued Development of Womanist Theology   81

   Discussion Questions   85

5. **Dialogue and Womanist Theology** 86

   Womanist or Black Feminist? Naming Ourselves   87

   Dialogue between Womanists and White Feminists   91

   Afrocentricity and Womanist Theology   93

   Black Theology and Womanist Theology   96

   Black Religious Traditions   98

   Dialogue with Students: Teaching Womanist Theology 101

   Womanist Thought in the Diaspora: Global Dialogue 102

   Discussion Questions   104

6. **Womanist Theology, Constructed** 105

   Suffering and Salvation   106

   Reconsidering Christology   113

   A Word about Womanist Biblical Scholarship   117

   Questions of God   118

   Personhood   121

   Discussion Questions   123

7. **New Challenges, Lingering Questions** **124**

    Pastoral Theology   124

    Ecumenical Dialogue   129

    Connections with Traditional African Religions   132

    Theology of Sexuality   138

    Ethnography and Art: Expanding Womanist Methods   140

    Conclusion   143

    Discussion Questions   144

Notes **145**

Bibliography **161**

Index **173**

Preface

The defined area of womanist theology is relatively new. This theological development is similar to the development of black theology, feminist theology, and other liberation theologies, yet distinct. It is both deconstructive and constructive and may employ a variety of disciplinary tools. Womanist theology offers opportunities for black women to feel fully participative in the theological processes and dialogues. Until "I" can state my realities as a human being, each person could assert, and state them within my own communal experiences of faith, I am limited to participating in theologies that draw from the ground of someone else's life. This individual need becomes critical for communities of people, that is, those who have common understandings and shared meanings.

In general, through womanist theology, one can observe how theologies are constructed. A sociodialogical dimension of theologies is operating in this black women's construction, along with the need for ongoing analysis. The development of womanist theology has the potential to shape personal and communal meaning in faith, to analyze church doctrines, and to challenge ecclesiastic operations.

Simply put, womanist theology is the systematic, faith-based exploration of the many facets of African American women's religiosity. Womanist theology is based on the complex realities of black women's lives. Womanist scholars recognize and name the imagination and initiative that African American women have utilized in developing sophisticated religious responses to their lives.

This book will give background for womanist theology. Both the objective visions of the theological enterprise and the subjective vistas of black women's faith experiences become windows to a clearer understanding of womanist theology. Yet, as an in-

troductory discussion, this text will not explain everything about
womanist theology.

There are black women living in every country of the earth with
many different experiences of the Divine. African American women
can be found in North, South, and Central America, and they have
vastly different experiences of life and faith. This text cannot cover
all these perspectives. The women in this book are primarily Christian and based in the United States. Nonetheless, there are other
faiths and nations where black women's religiosity needs exploration. This book will present a snapshot of womanist theology at
this moment, the beginning of the twenty-first century, but with the
understanding that such theology is subject to change as it grows.

Part I lays the foundations of womanist theology. Chapter 1
sketches some dynamics of black women's lives in order to make
connections with lived spiritualities and embedded theologies. It
responds to several questions. How are race, class, and gender
interwoven in black women's experiences? What is unique about
their experiences? What does this mean? Chapter 2 gives an
overview of distinctive components to be considered in the theological enterprise from perspectives of people of color. What are the
contours, dynamics, and methods of theology? How are theologies
constructed? The discussion of liberation theology situates womanist theology in a comprehensive view. Chapter 3 provides working
definitions for womanist theology that inform the rest of the book.
Questions framing this chapter are, What is womanist theology?
How does womanist theology express black women's lives?

The second part of the text provides a more focused look at
components and constructions of womanist theology. Chapter 4
considers the founding literature of womanist theology, looking at
signal texts and methods used in its development. Chapter 5 explores several of the ongoing dialogues that influence the shape
of womanist theology, including those between womanist scholars, feminists, students, and Afrocentrists. Chapter 6 turns to some
constructions of womanist theology — including salvation, black
women's suffering, christology, and personhood. Each of these
themes has benefited from the primary attention of womanist
theologians. Chapter 7 turns to the growing edges of womanist theology, which include womanist theological explorations of diverse

topics including pastoral theology, sexuality, traditional African religion, and ethnography and art.

In the process of assessing womanist theology, this text aims to make some connections between theory and practice. Womanist theology is not intended to exist in an academic vacuum: black women's experiences are forms and sources of scholarship. The words and actions of black women become an important component for two reasons. The first reason is tied to the methods of womanist theology, which remain connected and relevant to the women in the community. The second reason is tied to the first: as foundations are laid, demonstrations of womanist theology's resonance with the lives of black women affirm theories that are then developed. The community women noted in these chapters are primarily from one region of the country, the metropolitan area of Detroit. Some of the women were students, some are community activists, and others were part of a larger research project about healing and spirituality. These community women are not necessarily feminist or womanist in their own beliefs, but their words or actions indicate the wealth of information, already existent in black communities, from which womanists draw. The correlations between daily life and concepts, or practice and theory, themselves become a source of theological reflection.

Womanist theology aims for holistic links between faith and life. Readers of this text are invited to participate in this process of theological reflection through the discussion questions that are included at the end of each chapter.

Acknowledgments

Three groups were important in the development of this book. First, the twenty-plus participants and staff from the 1999–2000 American Academy of Religion/Lilly Foundation Teaching Workshop became colleagues and mentors during the year we worked together in the "Mining the Motherlode of African American Religious Life" sessions. This national group of scholars shared, inspired, and encouraged the development of teaching materials on topics of African American religion. This book is one product of that year's work. For reflections about teaching and black religious life, I thank my colleagues in the teaching workshop.

The second important group is the students with whom I have worked. They became dialogue partners in discussing womanist theology. Some of the discussion questions arose from these sessions. Some students suffered through early drafts of this manuscript and responded in writing. It was possible to include only a few of their often powerful and prayerful ideas in this book. I thank all my students for being my co-learners.

The third group is black women in the Detroit area. Azana and the Black Women's Health Project, Martha Jean "the Queen," and Jo Anne Watson are only a few of the women whose ideas and spirits infiltrate this work. These women exemplify the womanist spirit. I am grateful for the wisdom and encouragement I have received along the way.

My responsibilities for these gifts are to continue the processes of reflection and to share this wisdom with others.

Stephanie Y. Mitchem
University of Detroit Mercy
October 2000

Part I

What does it mean to be a black woman in the United States? What does it mean to be an African American woman and claim faith in a saving God? Would theological reflection somehow change in light of these meanings? How can theology interact with and enrich black women's lives? These questions are beginning points in the development of womanist theology.

The first three chapters begin to analyze the basic components of womanist theology. The realities of black women's experiences form the immediate context. The wider contexts of this womanist work are found in the disciplines of theology and the shifts brought about with the development of liberation theologies. The discussions of life and theology will lead to basic definitions of womanist theology.

Chapter 1

Black Women:
Race, Gender, and Class

The 1960s and 1970s were a time of turbulence in U.S. history: the fabric of what was presumed about American society was rent to disclose other social realities. Formerly colonized people — black, brown, yellow, red — began openly to question social relations, political power, and underlying meanings. Following the 1954 Supreme Court decision *Brown v. Board of Education,* legal segregation was outlawed. Since that time, through the Civil Rights, Black Power, feminist, and various white ethnic movements, socioeconomic shifts have been rapid and aided by advancements in technology. The discipline of theology also shifted: new voices with new realities pointed to new understandings of the Divine. Questions were formally raised about the ethical underpinnings of theology, theologies' constructions, and pastoral education. These questions led to new theological constructions which challenged many components of what is called Western or North Atlantic theology. Womanist theology was born in these historic and theological shifts.

There had been theological development from the perspectives of black men and from those of white women. However, neither category could speak for black women. Multiple social, political, and theological movements cleared a space for black women's voices to enter the ongoing theological conversations. Questions arose from black women's points of view, and by the late 1980s these voices were stronger and heard more clearly by other scholars. Cheryl Townsend Gilkes's sociological studies in the 1980s were critically important. She brought to light the many lay-

ers of meaning within that group of mostly black denominations
loosely termed the "black church." These layers hold meanings
for black women that were masked in the black theologies developed by men. Speaking of these different realities is central to
Gilkes's work:

> Since issues of social change were framed in religious terms,
> and religious perspectives focused on social change, black
> women participated in religious discourse even in settings
> where their right to preach was not affirmed.... Subordina-
> tion and subservience were evident problems, but not silence,
> isolation, and exclusion. Not only did black church women
> fashion important and necessary roles for themselves, they
> also had a powerful effect on religious discourse.[1]

Delores S. Williams was among other black women who defined the necessity of a theological analysis beyond that of white
women.[2] Feminism in general, and Christian feminism in particular, Williams charged, had been developed by white women to
focus exclusively on gender oppression. Feminists mainly identified
patriarchy — male control, dominance, and preference throughout
all institutions of society — as the center of gender oppression.
This focus only met the needs of white women, with their histories, and limited the relevance of feminism for black women in
the United States who had different experiences of domination.
Williams concludes that "demonarchy," not "patriarchy," would
be a better descriptive term, since men of any race, with the participation of white women, are involved in oppressing black women.
Williams and Gilkes were but two of the essayists entering the discussions that developed womanist theology. These and other works
are discussed in later chapters of this book.

Several book-length treatments in the late 1980s made womanist thought more readily available to the public. Katie G. Cannon's
dissertation was published and brought womanist ethical questions to the forefront. *Black Womanist Ethics*[3] resituated the
contexts of black women's ethical dilemmas. Jacquelyn Grant's
signal work, *White Women's Christ, Black Women's Jesus*,[4] set
out challenges to both white feminist and black male theologians.
Renita Weems's *Just a Sister Away*[5] connected biblical studies and

pastoral questions that black women face. With these authors, energetic explorations by womanists were brought to theological and ethical disciplines. Each of these works will be discussed in detail later. For now, it is important to stress that these thinkers came to understand that they were part of a long tradition of black women's religious thought. Their books, in conjunction with other essays, generated excitement at the possibilities of discussing God in black women's terms.

Womanist theology is about and for black women. Why is this type of theology needed? Both feminist and black theologies are, respectively, about women and black people. Aren't black women included in these discussions? Isn't womanist theology redundant? If theology includes discussion of the actions of God in human life, then exploration of the presence of God in the lives of black American women is necessary. Black women's lived experiences have structured their meaning-worlds that must be reflected in lives of faith.

Race, combined with gender, forms and informs the lives of black women. Additionally, socioeconomic dimensions of class and income, with categories of sexual preference and physical ability, layer the complexity of black women's experiences. This complex mixture generates particular faith responses and requires creative responses to daily life. Race, class, and gender all require exploration in order to understand how they combine and shape lives.

Dynamics of Gender: "Be a Lady"

How do African American women understand themselves as women? Some people in the United States, consciously or not, try to locate black women in their place and to confine their roles. "*All* black women are like ... " is a blank that some people readily complete with limiting answers. This type of thinking reduces the complexities of black women's lives to simple equations and is called essentialist thinking. Trying to identify all members of any group by some imagined essential nature is doomed to failure. Essentialist thinking creates stereotypes. Is it possible to discuss black women without resorting to essentialist terminologies?

One way to avoid this pitfall is to carefully consider and then state the contexts of black women's lives. Context refers to the real historical and contemporary aspects of life: where people live, what they eat, the political milieu, and child-rearing practices. Every aspect of life needs consideration in order to understand the context. These reality checks avoid the trap of abstracting life experiences into vague theories, which removes the diverse human element from the essentialized content. Avoidance of essential categories of womanhood is difficult in a society that has a consumer-driven notion of the feminine.

Other language than that of the dominant society is needed to discuss black women's apprehensions of themselves as women. Women of color have led contemporary scholarship in these efforts, moving away from the use of concepts that flatten all women's experiences into a single event. As an example, in the development of feminist concepts, black women's realities were lumped under an all-women-have-the-same-experience banner. However, black women still do *not* have the same experience as white women in America. Even as some areas of scholarship move toward fuller explorations of women's lives today, black women continue to be perceived as marginal in studies as well as American society. As historical conditions taught them, black women work to twist marginality to their and their communities' benefits.

Carla Peterson, a literary scholar, notes, "If positions at the center tend to be fixed, such is not the case for locations on the periphery, which can move and slide along the circumference. Indeed the black women I study repeatedly shifted approaches, strategies, and venues."[6] However, Peterson also notes that there is danger in the margins, which are not spaces of freedom, but locations of pain. It is in these margins that black women's conceptions of self as women reflect their mothers' lives, continue to be shaped, and are handed on to their daughters.

Marginalization implies the existence of hidden histories, even of black women's gender-role development. Beth Richie, a sociologist, offers a concept that brings light to African American women's sense of themselves as women. Richie studied black women who had been imprisoned and found some general themes. These women often committed crimes because they were attempting to be "good" women to their men. They would hold the bag of drugs or hold the gun, trying to fit into a supportive-woman role. Richie coined the term "gender entrapment" to explain this self-destructive belief system. Entrapment is a legal term that refers to a method of catching a person in crime by use of deliberate lures and situations that actually limit a person's free choice. In other words, gender entrapment happens because the women are lured by a desire to fit into a mistakenly perceived role of real and good women in American societies.[7]

Richie's construct of gender entrapment can be applied to African American women on a wider scale, not just those in prison. Gender entrapment is an issue with which black women in the United States must deal: it is embedded in the process of growing up. Being ladies becomes a crucible which affects black girls in particular ways as they are invited through social institutions to be "good" or shame the entire race of black people. Often, black women are judged, and harshly, by the way they present themselves. This is a remnant of a powerful Victorian-era belief that defined women as angels of the hearth: the home was their natural, proper sphere of influence. In this view, women did not work outside the home and waited to soothe the brows of the fathers, brothers, and husbands who did. Such ladies were to be protected by society, particularly their menfolk. The majority of black women have not had the economic ability to remain home-makers, often taking up the only work they could: keeping house for white women. Hence, beyond the time of enslavement, black women in America were not treated equally but were expected to still emulate the Victorian image to prove their worthiness.

There is another regional strain of this lady-mythology that also retains importance for African American women. The pre–Civil War Southern United States developed a plantation system as the basis of its economy. The plantation owners developed an American aristocracy. The enslaved Africans were the critical la-borers in building this world of privilege. Within this elite class, the Southern belle — the white, indulged daughter of the plantocracy — was held up as the flower of all that was feminine.

The Southern belle fantasy continues today, seen in the lingering glorification of the fictional character Scarlett O'Hara from Margaret Mitchell's 1938 novel. This form of the myth would have certainly influenced the enslaved Africans' beliefs about real American gender roles, particularly as the South was the point of entry for the majority of African Americans. Regardless of the route by which fantasies came to embed themselves in black and American mentalities, being a lady continues to hold power and becomes entrapment.

But there was another reason for any woman to fall into the trap. Throughout the years, attacks against black people by white citizens took many forms. Lynching was the most dreaded form of attack. It happened all too often to black men as well as to black women. Black women, and sometimes black men, feared the crime of rape as both sexes were viewed as sexual objects. Some older black women, particularly from the South, tell stories of white men forcing them to have sexual intercourse; to refuse or fight was to endanger the woman's entire family.

Beyond these forms of physical danger, a black person's or family's survival may have depended on public perception. Good social behavior was not a guarantee, but it was an attempt to safeguard self and community. Good black social behavior was balanced on a razor's edge of judgment that was sufficiently subservient and genteel. In this good behavior, how black women acted might become another thin barrier to protect self, family, and community. These ideas have become ingrained in many black communities and families.

The belief that black women must conform to a certain standard of being women, being real "ladies," was and is enforced within communities in many ways. One place of enforcement can be black churches, where the way a woman is dressed is a code for the way she is to be treated by the members of the church. One woman reported that an older member of her church, a deacon, brought her to task because she had had her hair cut very short due to illness. She had begun to wear her hair in a short, natural style. The deacon lectured her about hair as a "woman's crowning glory" and that proper hair maintenance was the duty of a Christian woman. He was advocating that she straighten her hair and look "normal" again. (Straightening hair requires chemicals or hot combs for many black women when the texture of their hair is naturally curly.) The woman was informed that her membership in the church community was in jeopardy; she chose to leave on her own. Too often, black women are given the message that they are just not good enough unless they *earn* respect and prove their communal worth, often by emulating white women. Black women are told through many means, from families to churches to schools, that they must conform to standards, that their reputations as women are open for public discussion, and that their own communities may stand in judgment. African American women can adopt these attitudes and enter the trap. They are then caught in the need to prove themselves, feeling the need to do more and to be best in any situation.

These issues about the gender entrapment of black women point to the relentless disempowering of black women that is part of a much wider patriarchal system. In *Sisters of the Yam: Black Women, and Self-Recovery,*[8] bell hooks stresses the necessity of self-care by black women, thereby becoming an advocate for black women's empowerment. She maintains that there are three aspects that need recognition to begin to care for self. These three are martyrdom, love, and wellness. These three aspects inform African American women's spiritualities as well.

Overworked and ill, bell hooks herself attempted to reduce her work load and lessen obligations. Her efforts were met with hostility:

> It seemed to me that if folks in this society have been socialized via racism and sexism to see black women as existing to "serve," it often follows that we should continue to serve even if we are sick, weary, or even near death.... We are grown women who are working to unlearn what I call "the black woman martyr syndrome."[9]

Self-sacrifice becomes the method of proving self-value as socially defined good ladies, who demonstrate moral character by being for others, with daily life circumscribed with the language of what "responsible girls" do, wear, or say. The subtext of this lan-

guage carries messages about the consequences of failure: to fail is
to also fail the entire race of black and brown people. Black women
often become the primary enforcers of these rules and roles and in
the process are trained to fear being true to self. bell hooks points
to the remedy for this tendency: "When we heal the woundedness
inside us, when we attend to the ... inner love-seeking, love starved
child, we make ourselves ready to enter more fully into community."[10] Attending to personal needs is not selfishness. Recognizing
the deep desire for love is a human necessity.

hooks has developed this theme of love, which holds particular importance for black women. "Many black women feel that
we live lives in which there is little or no love. This is one of our
private truths."[11] The experiences of feeling unloved and unappre-
ciated speak to the personal stresses through which black women
daily struggle. Yet the daily struggles of black women leave little
time for introspection. During an interview in Detroit, one black
woman described black women as "being like plants, we give ourselves up to seed."[12] Self-care is not a luxury for black women, as
gender entrapment makes it appear.

Because of these gender constructions, elaborate political ma-
neuvering comprises African American women's negotiations con-
cerning sex. These politics are in the private and public spheres of
black women's lives, at work and at home. Part of the maneuver-
ing is around stereotypes of sexually compulsive African American
women. Simply put, a sexually available black woman is a tramp
who cannot be socially redeemed. These views are continued in
some forms of rap music where girls and women are depicted
as greedy for money and sexual gratification. A related stereotype is about black women who are indolent recipients of welfare,
who raise their income by bearing many children and soaking up
taxpayers' dollars.

Because stereotypes of black women persist, it is sometimes too
easy to ignore the black woman sitting in the boardroom: even
though she is wearing a suit, she must be the cleaning woman.
The processes by which black women negotiate sexuality, in the
face of layers of stereotypes, become a deadly balancing act. Black
women learn not to take the events of life at face value and learn
to question everything. When does a request, from family or work

associates, cross the line into the stereotypical expectations? <u>Is this the time to ignore the insult or to take action</u>?

The private politics of sex can confound black women. Several black men who have achieved success, presumably born of black mothers, have made very public statements that they want nothing to do with black women and prefer <u>white or Asian women</u>'s company. <u>Black women are critiqued</u> for being too strong, castrating, unfeminine, or unsupportive. These critiques are not only from black men — black women chime into the chorus. As an example, Sharazad Ali, a black woman who wrote *The Blackman's Guide to Understanding the Black Woman*, stresses that black women in the United States lack femininity because of their disobedience and disrespect to black men. She establishes categories of black women, with the lowest being the educated one who secretly lusts after any white man. <u>Supporting a twisted idea of obedience, Ali instigates black men to slap their women in the mouth if they talk back or ask inappropriate questions</u>. These ideas are promoted by Ali for the good of the race and to strengthen black communities; she never recognizes that abused, ignorant women are detrimental to a community's quality of life.

These kinds of images and myths of *real* black women continue gender entrapment. A powerful question for reflection posed for African American women during retreats has been, When did you know you were a woman? Repeatedly, black women have reported that learning to say "no" to the demands of everyone else was a critical factor in determining their own identities. These women reported the painfully learned lessons that the fate of "the Race" of black peoples did not hinge on whether or not they took time for themselves.

Gender-role expectations and actual sexual behavior of African American women are in need of further study. Linda Kalof and Bruce Wade wrote in *The Journal of Black Psychology:*

> Given the large volume of work being done in the area of sexual attitudes and behavior, we lament the tendency for most researches to ignore race in their models of sexual behavior. Indeed, our study [on the influence of race and gender in sexual attitudes and sexual coercion] indicates that much can

be learned from more exploration into the world of Black women, who appear to embrace less traditional sex role attitudes, denounce rape myths, decry interpersonal violence, and reject adversarial sexual beliefs.[13]

These ideas will surface again in a later discussion of womanist theology of sexuality.

Dynamics of Race: "But You Are Black"

Race is a primary category that affects understandings of what it means to be whole persons. Whiteness is a social norm. "But you are black" becomes a mantra of limitation, reasoning that responds to the realities of racism. This mantra informs the personal reflections of Patricia Williams, a law professor:

> I remember with great clarity the moment I discovered that I was "colored." I was three and already knew that I was a "Negro" ... but "colored" was something else.... I still remember the crash of that devastating moment of union.... I have spent the rest of my life recovering from the degradation of being divided against myself; I am still trying to overcome the polarity of my own vulnerability.[14]

Race is a social construct, not a biological limitation. Racial concepts have constantly shifted: the word "race" itself was not incorporated into a dictionary until 1770. However, race remains a powerful concept. Race is a concept embedded today in American social worlds, a global, transnational, interclass process. Black women, men, and communities continue to expend enormous energy to combat the reduction of their humanity to the pathological lines of somebody else's bell curve. Historian Evelyn Brooks Higginbotham sharpens our focus when she define race as a

> "Metalanguage," since it speaks about and lends meaning to a host of terms and expressions, to myriad aspects of life that would otherwise fall outside the referential domain of race.... It makes hair "good" or "bad," speech patterns

"correct" or "incorrect." ... Race not only tends to subsume other sets of social relations, namely gender and class, but it blurs and disguises, suppresses and negates its own complex interplay with the very social relations it envelops.[15]

The concept of race developed historically to become a particular lens through which black women's bodies were defined. Black women's bodies were despised and exoticized when encountered by the European colonizers. These attitudes came with the slave ships to the colonies. Black women's bodies were viewed as grotesque and aesthetically displeasing, and, at the same time, as sexually powerful. In the white imagination, the black woman's body was seen as "public and exposed, ... an uninhibited laboring body that was masculinized. ... Feminine attributes and functions of the black female body were thus commonly represented in degraded terms as abnormal excessive sexual activity."[16] White women's bodies were the contrasting ideals against which black women were judged. Through a history of enslavement and abuse, concepts of race and gender were combined to further diminish the humanity of black women: the reproductive work of black women was reified. "Americans expect Black mothers to look like Aunt Jemima. ... American culture reveres no Black madonna; it upholds no popular image of a Black mother nurturing her child."[17]

Sociologist Cheryl Townsend Gilkes discussed her struggle to understand her own body as beautiful. A key moment for her was reading Alice Walker's definition of womanist. Gilkes recounts:

> In my personal encounter with Walker's definition, I stopped at "loves love and food and roundness." As a large, full-featured, dark brown African American women, I recognized a revolution in her call to love. Walker's emphasis remembered for me my own struggles with community and culture. My own experience and my understanding of the history of cultural humiliation embedded in American racism made it abundantly clear that these loves are not only a source of celebration and bonding in a human community, but also a protest against a culture that systematically assaults the self-esteem of African American women.[18]

[handwritten margin note: black women's bodies]

Many black women, learning to love their bodies, share these struggles. The size of lips or hips, the shade of skin, or straightness of hair still evoke stereotypes of black women in U.S. settings. Work is a particular area for black women where issues of race are transparent.

African Americans' lives are bounded by work, and women are gripped by assorted work-related stereotypes. For example, the fantasy of the "lazy black welfare mother" is just that — a fantasy which denies how hard black women work while it affirms how their work is undervalued. African American women have never been presented to the general public as needing protection of men or as delicate homemakers unfit to work outside the home, as were white women. Work, considered distasteful for "real ladies," has been part and parcel of most black women's lives. "Almost every black woman living in the United States has as her past the accumulated work of all her female forebears."[19] Black women have been both the producers in the labor force and the reproducers of the next generation of laborers.

Following the end of legal enslavement, the type of work that black women were expected to perform was generally in service of white people. Live-in domestics, day "girls," cooks, baby-sitters, and laundresses were common options for employment. A powerful look at the realities of work in black women's lives is found in the photographic text *The Face of Our Past,* edited by Kathleen Thompson and Hilary MacAustin.[20] This collection of photos and drawings of African American women through enslavement to the present often shows black women in poses of work. These working images are often overlooked and made invisible in American society. In reality, most black women, looking over their families' past, will find intimate awareness of some form of work that is tied to survival of the family and the spirit. The stories of black women and work need telling in order to be honest about American life and history. Some of the missing information is being completed in recent studies. For instance, *Parlor Ladies and Ebony Drudges: African American Women, Class, and Work in a South Carolina Community,* by Kibibi V. C. Mack,[21] gives a compelling snapshot of the work of black women in the small town of Orangeburg from the late-nineteenth through the twentieth centuries. Such historical studies are critically important in constructing womanist theology, for they define the real shape of black women's lives.

The contemporary experiences of black women and work need exploration as well. While there have been many advances in position and income, black women still have not reached income equity with black men or with white women, and all three of these groups lag behind white men. Race combines with gender to maintain the low pay and opportunities of black women. Two researchers concluded: "With regard to African American females, problems of gender discrimination are undoubtedly compounded by racial discrimination, thereby ensuring that, regardless of residential location, they occupy the lowest positions in the labor market."[22] Beyond the stresses of low income, many African American women continue to experience workplaces as downright hostile to their presence. For black women, psychological survival becomes as personally necessary as a paycheck. Carolyn Ratcliff, a black working woman, wrote of her experiences:

> The language of bureaucracy does not flow easily from my lips. I decline to dance the management tango. I do not have the self-confidence to attack the issues that plague myself and my coworkers. I am a black female that has been shown her designated station....I am not happy in this place yet the fear of encountering further wage disparities immobilizes me. My place is held by familiarity of salary, personnel, and routine. The fear of being without health insurance is only surpassed by the horror of being forced into a less desirable stereotype.[23]

Questions of Class

The myth of the American dream offers false hope that whoever works hard will succeed. The flip side of the same myth is an accusation that those who do not succeed are lazy and unwilling to work, for financial success is quietly held as a significant measure of social acceptance. This myth is important because it is one of the masks that hides the reality of class in America. Social class is real: the money Mike Tyson earns will still not erase class differences between him and, say, the Kennedy clan. Class realities are all around. Why do some private clubs attempt to exclude black people or women? Why do middle-class people want their children to marry "up" instead of "down"? Is a Harvard graduate more desired as a job applicant than the graduate of a community college? These are hidden facets of class in operation. Rogers M. Smith is a political scientist who analyzes the connections between race and class. He summarizes these distinctions: "Through merit, good fortune, or, most often, greater power, some people have controlled vastly more material resources and benefits, enjoyed higher status, and been especially commended in the prevailing social narratives about the character and value of different human lives."[24] All of the social, political, material, and status values given to a person or a group combine to create what is considered social class.

Most often class is used to refer to economic status. The great differences in wealth and income between black and white Americans create divides that inform a study by Andrew Hacker, *Two Nations: Black and White, Separate, Hostile, Unequal.*[25] His work painstakingly details the areas of the divisions between African Americans and white Americans. One area of particular importance to African American women is that of single mothers. Drawing from the 1990 U.S. Census figures, Hacker notes that women head 56 percent of black families, and 59.2 percent of those families live in central cities. Fifty-one percent of black children live only with their mothers, and 35 percent of black children's mothers have never been married.[26] These numbers put black women front and center on issues of class, particularly on the issue of the underclass.

Adolph Reed Jr., noted cultural critic and political scientist, indicates, "The underclass notion may receive the greatest ideological boost from pure sexism. For drug-crazed, lawless black and Hispanic men, the companion image is the so-called 'cycle of poverty,' which focuses on women's living and reproductive practices as the transmission belt that drives the cycle."[27] African American women are caught in class-determined traps by life circumstances.

The divisions noted by Hacker between black and white America are not just leftovers from the late twentieth century. Enslavement, followed by disenfranchisement, legal segregation, and the general denial of civil rights, kept black people from full social participation. "Race was intertwined with class as populations from various parts of the world were incorporated at different levels of the labor force,... producing a distinct experience for women of color."[28]

The story of black Americans and class is more than that of relationships with white America. There are also important dimensions to class internal to black communities. Historically excluded from the full economic and social benefits of their work, black Americans developed underground economic structures as part of their separate world; these communally developed structures also included notions of class in black communities. Educational level, skin color, speech patterns, and style of clothing became signs of being in a so-called better class of people within the black community. The efforts to improve life were tied to emulation of middle-class appearances and accumulation of money. As a result, class and status intertwine among African Americans while education and dress continue to serve as cultural capital in black communities. The way a woman dresses, the shine on a man's shoes, or the church a family attends can serve as intricate markers of the "better" class of black Americans.

In spite of formal or informal segregation, continuing high rates of poverty, and alternatively derived social status, class still has low visibility among African Americans, as bell hooks recounts from her childhood memories: "Everyone in our world talked about race and nobody talked about class....No one talked about the fact that no one had 'real' jobs at 1200 Broad Street, that no one made real money. No one called their lifestyle 'alternative' or utopian."[29] Even though class is often tied to income, financial discussions are often absent in black communities, as hooks relates from her life. "In my transition from the working class to the ranks of the upper-middle class, I was continually amazed by my lack of understanding about the way money works in this society."[30] The lack of information about investment, estate planning, and purchasing become real barriers to class mobility, especially since black women head a significant percentage of households.

Blacks look investment planning and financial help

The complexities around class issues in black communities open up painful discussions of who black folk think we are and who we hope to be. The end of legal segregation in 1954 created some new possibilities and new realities in black communities. Today there are both more and fewer opportunities. Class stratification in black communities has reached new levels of sophistication and complexity and is played off against race. The existence of a few prominently placed black women and men creates the popular belief that success obliterates the racial barriers that block entrance to the middle class.

Regardless of internal operations of class within black communities, there remain other dynamics with the wider U.S. society that continue to shape black women's reality. In *Fighting Words: Black Women and the Search for Justice*, Patricia Hill Collins sociologically analyzes the multiple facets of black women's lives today. Collins's first chapter is titled "The More Things Change, the More They Stay the Same." According to Collins, the status quo is ensured by a new politics of containment that holds black women in "place":

> Because working-class and poor Black women are members of an intensely raced group, the domestic violence, sexual promiscuity, strained family relations, and other personal difficulties that they encounter in large part because of their race and economic class position become highly visible. ... Surveillance [of middle-class black women] operates via strategies of everyday racism whereby individual women feel that they are being "watched" in their desegregated work environments. Surveillance also functions via media representations that depict the success of selected high-achieving Black women.[31]

As a result of the internal dynamics of class, and surveillance by the wider society, black women live a reality of exclusion that adds more layers to the complexities that they face every day. The amount of energy needed to deal with dynamics of race, gender, and class is tremendous.

Race with Gender with Class:
Connecting the Dots

Black women continue to struggle against misrepresentation in a society that still undervalues who they really are. The black feminist Michele Wallace terms this experience "invisibility blues":

> What most people see of the black woman is a void, a black hole that appears empty, not full. The outsider sees black feminist creativity as a dark hole from which nothing worthwhile can emerge and in which everything is forced to assume the zero volume of nothingness, the invisibility, that results from the intense pressure of race, class, and sex.[32]

Even though celebrity icons like Oprah seem to signify that "success is possible," black women who are not Oprah daily become invisible; they are expected to be workers: expected to hold the broom or care for the child or type the memo or cook the meal. Often black women who do not work in service or pink-collar occupations are viewed as the oddity. A black woman teacher was informed by an older white woman, "I never knew black people could talk as good as you do." Another black woman told of the many times that she would walk into a room with her white secretary and most people assumed that the secretary was the boss. These daily experiences of oppression take a tremendous toll. They are not singly race- or class- or gender-derived oppressions, but a combination that generates a central facet of black women's experience. Analysis of these ideas has become a focus of black women intellectuals and marks one of their major overall contributions to contemporary scholarship.

Patricia Hill Collins states that black women "inhabit a sex/gender hierarchy in which inequalities of race and social class have been sexualized."[33] Leith Mullings, an anthropologist, synthesizes the ideas of several theorists:

> It is important to make the point that race, class, and gender are not additive categories; rather, they are interlocking, interactive, and above all relational ones.... For the majority of African American women, race, class, and gender are the an-

alytic constructs that have the greatest explanatory power in interpreting and predicting their conditions of existence. As axes of stratification, they are fluid systems that intersect in different ways for different populations at different historical periods.[34]

As intellectuals attempt to maintain a tridimensional analysis, that is, incorporating race, class, and gender, individual women continue as invisible in American society. Janice N. Tillman, a college student reflecting on these ideas, wrote "Who Am I?" to express her "invisibility blues":

> Am I the grass under your feet?
> The wind that blows over your head?
> Am I the black spot you can't remove?
> Or am I the blockage you can't get through?
> If I am not the grass, why do you walk on me?
> If I am not the blowing wind, why don't you
> Pay any attention to me?
> If I am a black spot you can't remove, why
> Don't you accept my color?
> And if I am what is blocking your way, why don't
> You allow me the tools I need to move forward
> In my life?
> If who I am to you means nothing, let me be
> Who I am to me.[35]

Race with gender with class becomes a centrifuge that creates new meanings for black women. However, black women resist these limiting definitions, growing new meanings that resonate with their realities and hopes. This is called agency, referring to the ability of a person or community to work on their own behalf, within or in spite of existing social institutions. Sometimes the term "agency" is used to refer to a person's ability to make decisions and act; however, the concept is used here in a slightly broader form. Agency is used here to refer to the visioning gift that sees beyond simple tasks of survival. This kind of visioning will help a person to define the importance of activism on behalf of self and community. Agency refers to the dual processes by which black people may work for as well as against social structures and institutions. For example, Michele Wallace, responding to black women's invisibility, finds that giving voice to black women's realities is a necessity: "Only with those voices — written, published, televised, taped, filmed, staged, cross-indexed, and footnoted — will we approach control over our own lives."[36]

Agency also stands against the internalized self-hatred found among some African Americans. Self-hatred becomes embedded into a group through its adoption of prevailing negative images. For African Americans, this process establishes another dialogue that is internal to the black community. Self-hatred is related to the concept of hegemony — the domination and control that white Americans have been able to exert over black Americans. While adoption of the gender-role definitions of the dominant society may have been geared toward helping black communities survive in the past, contemporary experiences create new needs. "Many of the issues that we continue to confront as black people — low self-esteem, intensified nihilism and despair, repressed rage and violence that destroys our physical and psychological well-being — cannot be addressed by survival strategies that have worked in the past."[37] At minimum, a tridimensional analysis of sex, race, and class oppressions should lead toward new language and activism, compared with the strategies of the 1860s or 1960s. Scholarship that focuses on race *with* gender *with* class means that the entire African American community's life is involved. This idea of scholarship will involve discussion and dissension within black communities and lead to new social action.

[margin note: what used to work to help black commun. does not work any more.]

It is not a new phenomenon in the United States that black people are learning new ways to name themselves, and it is not new that black women are integrally involved in the process. At issue in the discussions is the very value of black life. Delores Williams, as a womanist theologian, identifies "survival and quality of life" as central:

> The term quality of life...refers to persons, families and/or communities attempting to arrive at well-being through the use of, search for and/or creation of supportive spiritual, economic, political, legal or educational resources....In the

context of much black American religious faith, survival struggle and quality of life struggle are inseparable and are associated with God's presence with the community.[38]

African American women often express their commitment to the entire community by working for the health for all members. In their actions, the race-gender-class interconnections are made visible. A community activist in the city of Detroit is an example. Jo Anne Watson has worked against racism with the Young Women's Christian Association and worked for justice with the National Association for the Advancement of Colored People. Today she works for reparations for black Americans' enslavement. For this, she is a leader in the National Coalition for Reparations for Black Americans. Some people would name Watson's efforts futile, however, she clearly identifies her work as being on behalf of the entire black community. She is a religious woman, peppering her conversations with faith statements, so that it is clear that God is central in her life and actions. In conversation, she refuses to allow any stereotypical, limiting, or derogatory language about black women to slide by without her correction of the speaker. There are many Jo Anne Watsons throughout black communities.

Agency is a force for transformation for Africans Americans generally, as well as for womanists. Resistance against narrow definitions and life-destroying constrictions is a form of agency that informs the religious traditions of black people. Religious centers have been subversive training grounds for many black women and men. Gathering up and drawing from histories, social constructions, activisms, and faith, womanist theology responds to the unique realities of black women.

Becoming Womanists

The unique experiences of black women emphasize the reality that life has social structures that develop in different ways over time and in different locales. These social structures become the routes through and on which humans, in faith, construct theologies. Further, human beings are limited by an era, place, culture, and history. This is a humbling fact because it follows that human definitions cannot limit God's meanings: we are constantly learning. The contemporary scholarly work of women, people of color, and African American women shifts perspectives and forces people out of their comfort zones. Womanist theology shifts the perspectives and asks more questions. Where is God in the experiences of black women? By what name should this God be called? What does it mean to live a life of faith? How should black women respond to God's call?

Womanist theology starts with analysis of roles assigned to African American women by their families and the dominant culture, the persistent stereotypes about black women, the combination of race with gender, and recognition of diversity among women. For black women to do this analysis is, in itself, empowering as we discover truths about ourselves. The skill of naming personal truths is drawn from black women's networking traditions and is part of womanist theology. As happens in sometimes subtle, sometimes blatant, ways, black women participate in a revolution when they reach for power in the face of a nonsupportive system.

The recognition of personal truths and communal networking are part of a wider web of values that black women can claim. Recognizing what is valuable is important and can be uncovered with the question, What is life-giving to you? When black women name the life-giving, they move beyond merely reacting to creating. African American women have not accepted stereotypes or socially imposed limits but have acted as agents on their own behalf wherever or however possible. It is important to give name to values because these serve as lenses through which society is analyzed. For instance, differences in child-rearing practices or the use of money or church attendance can reflect deeply held values.

In addition, through analysis of life experiences in dialogue with other African American women, some black women come to name themselves womanists. JoAnne Marie Terrell, a womanist theologian, has recently written an extensive study of the meaning of the cross in black religious symbology. Her in-depth discussions are clearly done as a womanist; the very process of naming herself such is part of her analysis:

One does not get to be a womanist by virtue of her blackness and femininity. Nor does one become a womanist simply because one reads, understands and makes the appropriate adjustments in her life. The lived-world struggle to appropriate self-love as the operative principle is formidable. <u>Black women entering the womanist enterprise commit to exploring further the contradictions that shape their collective and personal lives in the spirit of critical inquiry and in the spirit of hope.</u>[39]

 Becoming a woman 1st

These processes of growth become the marrow of womanist theology.

Discussion Questions

1. What is meant by the term "gender entrapment" and how can it be understood to impact the lives of black women?

2. What are some stereotypes of African American women that still exist today? Use one current film or television program to discuss the stereotypes you name.

3. Discuss how race combines with gender for black women. From your own experience or observation, give one real life example of this combination. If you have never experienced or observed this combination, discuss why that is so.

4. Trace your own history of being "raced" or "gendered." When did you know you were a given race or gender? How did you find out? Did it make a difference in your life? Focus on a single incident which highlights either race or gender awareness.

Chapter 2

Constructing Theologies

To connect African American women's experiences in the United States with the development of womanist theology, an understanding of the components of theology itself is needed: its contours, its dynamics, and its tasks and methods. In the previous chapter, discussion of black women's identities raised the idea of *construction* — a concept that indicates that historical streams converged to shape contemporary perceptions of African Americans, both men and women. Those streams were both internal and external to black communities, tied with the politics and philosophies of the times, reflected in families and churches. The resulting ideas became embedded in the fabric of societies, and a given community's members grew to assume these constructions were "natural" and "right." Thinking through how social concepts developed requires that intellectuals, formally or informally, undertake tasks of deconstruction of the roots and results of ideas. These analyses are part of twentieth-century scholarship and richly inform the work of a variety of social scientists: sociologists, anthropologists, historians, philosophers, and so on.[1]

In theology, these analyses have yielded liberation theologies. *A Black Theology of Liberation,* by African American theologian James Cone, was published in 1970. In 1973, Peruvian theologian Gustavo Gutiérrez's *A Theology of Liberation* was published in the United States.[2] Their uses of the term "liberation" moved theological discourse into simultaneous processes of deconstructing and revisioning theology from the views of people of color. Womanist theology is one form of liberation theologies. The constructions of Western or North Atlantic theologies can be contrasted to liberation theologies. This chapter will explore these differences in order to reach a working set of definitions that inform the constructions of womanist theology.

Contours of Theology

Theology is powerful, and its notions become embedded in social frameworks. Deconstruction of theologies is difficult, as the ideas can be presented as "God's designs," rather than the constructions of human beings. An extended example of this difficulty will illuminate the complexities involved in the constructions of theology. Specifically, the theological developments that denied African people their humanity ran parallel to the historical processes of their enslavement, highlighting the human factors in religious constructions.

The people in the complex web of shipping lines, trade routes, and governments who enslaved black people in the sixteenth and seventeenth centuries simultaneously developed ideas to justify those processes, beginning with denials of the very humanity of the Africans. Had African people mated with chimpanzees? With gorillas? Did the shapes of black people's heads or the sizes of genitalia prove they were a different species of humans? Skin color in particular was believed to be sign of God's curse against black people. This theological idea was interwoven with many other developments in science and philosophy that further denigrated black people. The interrelated concepts grew, fueled by philosophers like Jean-Jacques Rousseau and John Locke; by European beliefs in the myth of "progress"; by the equation of civilization with European lifestyles; by the growth of nationalism; by the practice of capitalism; and by the development of theories of evolution. All these were thrown into high gear by the placement of science and reason as new and verifiable gods of modern thinking.

These ideas grew as the United States and European countries expanded their control of other parts of the world through colonization. Though colonization began in the sixteenth century, the nineteenth century ushered in an intense period of Western conquest and control termed "modernity." Human beings were defined in relationship to their participation in Western ideals, and the science of the times was used to classify people and their cultures. The losers in these constructions were people of color.

Additional questions about the humanity of black people can be found in the field of anthropology, important because of links with theological concepts. Western anthropology of religion considered the religious thought of African people and generally dismissed these complex beliefs as ignorant, childlike superstition. A thorough analysis of dehumanizing beliefs by various writers and thinkers, such as W. E. B. Du Bois, from the late nineteenth through the twentieth centuries served as a counterpoint; however, these countervoices were often unheard and marginalized. Racist ideologies continued to grow.

Christian missionaries of many denominations accompanied the European explorers and met and blessed the slave ships, even as mainstream denominations financially benefited from the slave trade. Besides Bibles, white Christian evangelists carried Western cultures. Enslavement of black people was viewed as part of a God-given natural, social order, and North Atlantic Christian theology came to justify the misconceptions and unjust treatment of people of color.

Robert E. Hood traced the historical roots of these misinterpretations of Christianity as necessarily white/European.[3] In *Begrimed and Black: Christian Traditions on Blacks and Blackness,* Hood surfaced concepts that were found in Greek, Roman, and African thinking before the Christian era and that continued through the periods of colonization. Hood also evidenced the impact of negative views in the writings of political theorist Charles-Louis Montesquieu, whose work influenced the framers of the American Revolution. Hood cited a 1748 text by Montesquieu:

> It is hardly to be believed that God, who is such a wise Being, should place a soul, especially a good soul, in such a black ugly body. . . . It is impossible for us to suppose these creatures to be men, because, allowing them to be men, a suspicion would follow that we ourselves are not Christians.[4]

A theology that incorporates a justification of enslavement would certainly not celebrate the goodness of black people.

Black people have actively resisted theological constructions of a God that created or cursed them for enslavement by superior white people. In 1829 David Walker wrote *An Appeal to the Coloured Citizens of the World, but in Particular, and Very Expressly, to Those of the United States of America.* Walker's text was passionate with sarcasm:

> [W]e, (colored people) and our children are *brutes!!* and of course are, and *ought to be* SLAVES to the American people and their children forever!! to dig their mines and work their farms; and thus go on enriching them, from one generation to another with our *blood* and our *tears!!!*[5]

Walker drew from history and Christian Scripture to denounce the activities of white enslavers and false preachers of the gospel. "What can the American preachers and people take God to be? Do they believe his words? . . . Or do they believe, because they are whites and we blacks, that God will have respect to [*sic*] them?"[6] Walker encouraged white people to repent and end enslavement, and he exhorted black people to rise up and throw off the yoke of the oppressors. David Walker died mysteriously in 1830.

Walker's theological statement analyzed enslavement and perceptions of black people. His writing highlighted the ways religious thought can become embedded with values of the dominant society. Religion's influence in shaping society's thought — and Walker's attempt to surface another perspective — demonstrates again that theology is indeed powerful.

Many traditions of Western or North Atlantic theology incorporate implicitly and explicitly stated negative ideas about black people. These beliefs go hand in hand with ideas that European cultural perspectives are superior and universally true: those who deviate are considered uncivilized. Indeed, Western theological perspectives are so embedded that some black congregations have adopted these and other inherently racist beliefs. To picture Jesus as only a blond, blue-eyed figure has been held up by some black theologians as symbolic of black people's self-negation. The Shrines of the Black Madonna and the Nation of Islam are religious movements from within black communities that are invested in countering the religious self-hatred of black people.

While race remains problematic for black people in the Americas in general, gender is an additional problem, deeply felt by black women. If black women press for gender justice, are efforts for racial justice weakened? Michele Wallace's *Black Macho and the Myth of the Superwoman,* widely published in 1980,[7] was condemned, not surprisingly, by some black men as a male-bashing treatise that destroyed a surface-level black unity. Wallace's book began a deconstruction project both of the ways black men are seen in American society and of the expectations that the men place on women. Wallace also analyzed ways that black girls are raised to fear being seen as strong women who figuratively castrate black men. Wallace wrote of the ways that black women are seen as the downfall of the black race: "By the time I was fifteen, there was nothing I dreaded more than being like the women in my family.... All of them were haughty about having made their own way."[8]

This discussion had been heightened by the speculations of the Moynihan Report a few years earlier, which had its own ignominious role in blaming a mythical black matriarchy for the destruction of families due to preventing black men from being "masculine."[9] African American men and women were caught in a cycle of proving their worth through adherence to the white, middle-class gender-role conformity that has been toxic to black sexuality. When women are strong, do men lose "manhood"? When women are assertive, are men disrespected? Can the economic success of black women destroy racial unity? Does the very existence of the family depend on members' fulfillment of middle-class, nuclear roles? These questions are framed here with a slant to demonstrate their speciousness, yet possible answers hold emotional sway within black communities. Looking over Wallace's book from the perspective of the twenty-first century, these questions still point to the realities and deep-seated fears of black women in the United States. Considered theologically, another question can be raised: Can the presence of God be found in black women who bear social stigmas and live stereotypes?

The contours of theology are shaped by everyday lives. In spite of thinkers who present ideas as if theology is a discipline removed from the ebb and flow of human life, reality continues to intrude. Each human being, including the theologian, is part of this world, breathing in cultural, social, economic, and political meanings. Theologians, all of whom are rooted in a particular time and place, must address issues of faith, holiness, and salvation.

Dynamics of Theology

If the shape of a theology is determined in relationship to the times in which it is constructed, then each construction will stand in conversation with those times. Some theological constructions support the status quo; some stand in challenge to the times. There are many ways in which a theological structure can support the normative, dominant perspectives in any society. For example, the already-cited quote by Montesquieu questions whether God could have created good souls in ugly black bodies. He presented a theological dilemma: either black people are without a human soul, *or* the enslavers are not Christian. Answering this theological problem in one way becomes a rationale for the enslavement of black people; answering it differently calls for repentance by those who call themselves Christian.

The human process of theology surfaces human responses. It is not surprising that the plantocracy of the South did not want to hear any theology but that which proved enslavement was a good thing. Kenneth Stampp, a historian, wrote of the ways that religion was used against the enslaved Africans:

> Through religious instruction the bondsmen learned that slavery had divine sanction, that insolence was as much an offense against God as against the temporal master. They received the Biblical command that servants should obey their masters, and they heard of the punishments awaiting the disobedient slave in the hereafter.[10]

The planter class clearly benefited financially from enslavement and would have lost money from a different theological construction.

A way to think about these different views is in terms of paradigms. While the concept has been overused, it still offers

a method of considering the multileveled miscommunications between groups of people, in this case, people who operate from
paradigms of Western traditions and those who do not. The ones
who do not are often people of color. Colonization and economic control moved Western thought into positions of dominance
throughout the world. This dominance gave a comforting illusion
of unity and uniformity. But the world has become smaller with
technology, and nations have re-formed into different blocs and
alliances. Since the 1950s, with civil rights and slow expansions
and changes in some areas of scholarship, what had been glossed
over in Western views as nonessential came glaringly into focus:
women and people of color see the world differently. The operative
paradigms of marginalized groups are different from those of the
dominant perspective. Ignored and suppressed ideas began to be
explored. This also led to serious reconsideration of Western traditions themselves from the perspectives of black, brown, red, and
yellow people and women of all colors. Scholars became aware
that ideas understood as universal were, in fact, constructed and
exclusive of many people's realities. Western constructions have
historically privileged the perspectives of certain groups as right,
good, and natural to the exclusion of others' perspectives. This
consideration of the historical preferential treatment of one group's
ideas over all others provides an important lesson: some community stands at the center of a theological construction; sociocultural
assumptions are embedded in the construction; some group is privileged in and benefits from that construction. In other words, no
single construction can be all things to all people.

Today, these same dynamics are at work, sometimes in less blatant forms. It is not transparent which group is privileged or who
benefits from a given theological construction. Who determines
when God is truly on "our" side? Analysis of the current world
demands an ability to critique that which is understood as normal
and those aspects of society that are "the way things have always
been." Gender or racial roles have certain socially constructed
boundaries, but they are not the only constructions thought of as
normative. A striking example is brought to public attention by
disability rights activists who challenge the view that being able-
bodied (over which we have little choice) is the best or right way to

be fully human. A willingness to risk all that is ideologically held dear is needed for genuine cross-cultural dialogue. This requires openness to other perspectives — such as those of women, people of color, the disabled, and the poor — in liberative theological analyses.

Much formal theological construction occurs and is validated in the realm of higher education. Yet academic circles have been slow to recognize the intellectual validity of members of the community who were not traditionally part of the academy, and consequently slow to vigorously support research from the perspectives of people of color. Instead an intellectual hangover of a single American culture based on a single American experience continues. Nostalgia for a reality that never existed has captured the American imagination. At any university, these same social tensions exist among faculty, students, staff, and alumni; arguments about affirmative action or campus diversity are common today. Most scholars have been trained in a hierarchicalized view of knowledge, where some information has been deemed better, good, worse, and so on. Scholars easily make a commitment to maintain the status quo because financial and social rewards are built into the system. This is logical, for the status quo offers an orderly, safe, and closed system of viewing the world.

Black theology has had a presence in the academy since the 1960s. Womanist theology is even more recent, arriving in the late 1980s. The acceptance of black and womanist theologies has involved a series of struggles on multiple levels throughout the academy. As is true in other academic disciplines, barriers are encountered by theologians who attempt to step outside the conceptual world of the status quo. Liberation theologies, of which womanist is one, challenge some aspects of North Atlantic theological traditions. Discomfort with acknowledging this different theological strand can bring some scholars and pastors to just ignore it — it might go away. One African American woman who wanted to study womanist theology contacted several schools. Finally, she encountered one that had at least heard of it, but was told that such study was extracurricular. The implications were clear: womanist theology is not "real" and is superfluous to genuine academic enterprise.

This one woman's experience is not unique. Mary Romero and Debbie Storrs write of experiences of women of color who have undertaken research:

> Rosa described a faculty member's response.... "I said my name is such and such and my dissertation is going to be on the labor force participation of Latinas in (X) city. And the same professor just cracked up. He said 'What? Latinas? Is that sociology?' "...Another woman received similar messages.... "They (faculty) were telling me that it (the study of an ethnic group) was too subjective and I should learn to do more things, be more objective and cover a broader area."[11]

These tensions are part of the development of scholarship, which is part of all the shifts in the world. Ending the colonial status of Asian and African nations by European countries and strengthening civil rights protections for all people in the United States have created a climate in which scholarship changed as well. The mid–nineteenth and early twentieth centuries ushered in a frame of scholarly and academic reference known as modernity. By the mid–twentieth century, many modernist assumptions were challenged with a new referential framework called post-modernity. More detail on these important frameworks will assist in understanding changes in the discipline of theology.

Modernity and postmodernity are ways of thinking, general mind-sets that solidified over time. Modernity in general is understood to have begun in the 1800s, with the expansion of European colonization. It was fueled by philosophical positions that gave primacy to rationality and that structured all humans into hierarchies. The processes of defining the genus and species of all beings and things and of dissecting everything into the smallest components had advantages for many societies and led to many scientific advances that are part of the modern mindset. Nations such as the United States were established during this time, and nationalism grew. Churches lost some of their unquestioned authority in matters of science and statehood as humanism moved into a competitive relationship with religion. The industrial revolution made many men rich with side effects of sweatshops and air pollution.

Academic disciplines such as psychology and sociology began to sketch their boundaries at the beginning of the twentieth century.

This same modernist thinking established categories of races, classes, and other distinctions between human beings that remain embedded in communities. The category of race established the normative human being and the "other" simultaneously. Stuart Hall, a British sociologist, explains "othering" as a process:

> It is part of the long history of the dialectics of "othering": these are all others of one kind or another, those that weren't othered through slavery were othered through colonialism or othered through imperialism. And some were othered through all three. Each of these people cling to the particular homes and the identities that were formed through those histories.[12]

Times began to change in the mid–twentieth century. New thinkers challenged constructions of "othering" and introduced new voices into academe. Postmodernist frames of reference began deconstruction of the old categories of race, gender, and class differences with aims of challenging oppressions. Yet postmodernism has its own problems. The processes of deconstruction have led some scholars to prematurely announce the end to all oppressive categorizations of human beings. The deconstruction of the concept of race, for example, only obscures that nothing has really changed. Cornel West states:

> These *deracialized* discourses about modernity are disarming and deceptive in the face of the persistence of white supremacy here and abroad. The denial of race in these "color-blind" perspectives about the modern past or the postmodern present is the intellectual counterpart of the denial of the legacy of white supremacy in our society and world. As long as race is simply added to the *central* dynamics of modernity or glibly marginal to the emergence and sustenance of American society, this lethal denial persists.[13]

These complexities inform the theologies of people of color, the "others."

Defining Theology

The definition of theology is not benign, but carries its own weight of culture and commitment. Theology informed the pastoral lives of churches even as churches played roles throughout the history of colonizing people. Whether the language was of manifest destiny or providence, the promised land or the white man's burden, religious undertones infused expansion and colonization. Certain strands of thought within Western theology powerfully justified these movements. North Atlantic theologies are, in the main, influenced by Greco-Roman philosophical traditions that (1) make sharp distinctions between body and soul; (2) give preference to the spiritual/mental over the physical; and (3) believe that a universal, one-size-fits-all theology is possible.

Developing from the fourth century of the common era to this day, the emphasis on the separation of body and soul was accompanied by belief in a hierarchy of one over the other: usually the spirit is good, the body is evil, and the spiritual realm is preferred over the earthly. This culturally derived perspective about the body remains in the theologies of many churches. However, many people, such as sub-Saharan Africans, did not subscribe to such a view of the body.

Understanding the body and soul as discrete, embattled entities serves to isolate the human person. As a result of this perspective, all life can be viewed as disconnected fragments that can be hierarchically arranged, flowing from ideas of the body as "bad" and the soul as "good." The rugged individual of the North Atlantic tradition contracts socially with a group for personal protection, but conceivably could leave the group; individuality is more important than communality. In this Western tradition, the idea of the philosopher Descartes reigns: "I think therefore I am." The emphasis on the individual, particularly human will, is a well-developed note in Western theological traditions. This is different from attitudes toward the relationship of body and soul in other cultures. As a contrast to Descartes's notion, John Mbiti notes a proverb from African philosophy: "I am because we are."[14] In this African thought tradition, the person is not a separate, isolated individual but is rooted in a community that creates a personal identity.

Western traditions generally viewed the body itself as weak or evil: the physical lessened the ability to reason or commune with God. The body was believed unclean and tending toward ungodliness. After all, the body died while the soul did not, and this proved the matter. Women's bodies particularly, bound by menses, childbirth, and the sin of Eve, seemed to represent all that was messy and physical and decayed. Becoming Christian, in some religious traditions informed by such theologies, demanded denial of the physical in all its aspects including bodily functions, sensuality, and pleasure. Having too good a time was, surely, some form of sin, so some Christians' worship-expressions demanded a kind of insensate joylessness. Further, the division of body and soul and the preference for the spiritual over the physical were believed to be universal for all civilized, sophisticated, higher reasoning people. This Western universal was, in actuality, laden with the cultural biases and perspectives of the dominant European peoples.

In the development of dominant Western theologies through much of the twentieth century, the voices of people of other traditions were excluded, except as examples of the "primitive" or "exotic." In spite of such resistance by European cultures, people of color never ceased thinking theologically. One example is found in the multiple ways voodoo developed across different national groupings, reflecting retentions of African religious forms. These African-derived forms, like those of other people of color, were dismissed from "legitimate" theological consideration as the North Atlantic views had the power to dominate college classrooms.

This domination of Christian theology by Western tradition has had two results relevant to our current discussion. First, a range of correct theological methods was developed and established. Either deliberate heresy or blind ignorance was the verdict on the religious thought of anyone who operated outside these methods. Theologians operating within this Western perspective became apologists for the status quo (evidence of God's blessings, of course). Second, Christian churches promoted cultural domination from the pulpit. "A dialectic between evil and sin, eroticism and carnality, sanctity and magic has characterized beliefs and images of blackness in Christian thought. This same dynamic has also eroded the claims of racial inclusiveness in Christian thought as a theological foundation."[15]

Western Christianity has been uniquely paranoid-schizophrenic and obsessive-compulsive in approaching different cultures. On the one side, there was hope of embracing the perspectives of those designated "others"; on the other side, a European cultural bias simultaneously expected a change from heathenish ways. The result was the sometimes forced conversion of people believed to be inferior. The effort to convert the heathens was accompanied by a sexual fascination with and use of people of color. Black women were even more exoticized. Emilie M. Townes cites one example:

> The body of the indentured servant, Sarah Bartmann, exemplified this spectacle of female body parts. Dubbed the "Hottentot Venus," Bartmann's naked body was repeatedly displayed [in Paris] over a period of five years between 1810 and 1815. When she died, at the age of twenty-five, she was dissected by her admirers and in the name of science.[16]

The negative views toward people who think in non-Western modes are still present across the globe. These views are insidiously resistant and resilient. Robert Hood noted that theological language has, in the main, been corrected to include people of color. But, beyond that, "Blackness and black complexions...have always carried baggage in Western civilization and the Christian tradition that counter this theologically correct interpretation."[17] This is the climate in which many people of color still do theology.

A main focus within contemporary theology is the recovery and restatement of the subjugated strands of human meaning, particularly those of women and people of color. This process has been one of the most significant shifts in theological thinking since the late 1970s. One adjective that covers many of these theologies — including black, feminist, and womanist — is liberative. Liberation theologies differ in that each speaks to the particular realities of a group of people who have been silenced. What meanings do they give to religion, to God, to life? As questions are raised and answers are explored, the variety of responses highlights distinctions among different groups of people. The result is a complex frame that liberates the definitions of theology itself.

Defining Liberation Theologies

Liberation theologies have developed from the particular perspectives of people who were viewed as outsiders to the closed circles of Western thought. This section will consider the ideas of several liberation theologians in order to present defining aspects of liberation theologies.

Luis G. Pedraja, a Hispanic theologian, maintains there is more to theology than a mere "cognitive enterprise." The theologies we construct communicate with God and with other people about who God is to us. Pedraja calls for a holistic view of theology, with the thoughts, actions, and feelings of each human person and the entire community fully engaged. The communal aspect is critical: "A good theology must speak beyond the closed academic circles of universities and scholars and speak the language of the people and empower their faith."[18] This holistic view that includes language and the ways we use it is important in how we think about theology. Pedraja explains how significant language is: "Marginalized groups and theologies carry qualifiers, such as 'Hispanic' theology, while those who are in power simply see their theologies and experiences as universal and thus as the normative or universal expression of theology."[19]

Pedraja presents several defining characteristics of theology. It is more than cognitive, and it reaches for holistic understandings that involve the whole person. Theology is how we communicate *with* God and how we communicate *about* God. As a human process, theology must consider the uses of language. The discovery of this power of naming human experiences of the Divine is always grounded in a cultural context. What Pedraja points to as important for Hispanic theology is also important for other people of color, and many of the same themes mark the work of other theologians.

Ivone Gebara is a feminist theologian from Brazil. She noted that theology can begin

> with shared experience from oral transmission, from the simple fact of sharing life. I believe this way of doing theology is what is most representative of the popular milieus.... Dis-

course dealing with the important issues of life is the heart of
every theology. God's life is related to the life of humankind,
and the life of humankind is related to God.[20]

Theology begins not in a classroom but in living life. This is
a departure from ideas of theology as controlled by the academy.
Now the theological enterprise can locate itself in Gebara's Brazilian communities and, by extension, on the home ground of any
people. Theology is not the exclusive property of the elite. Both
Gebara and Pedraja note the importance of grounding theology in
real life experiences.

Chung Hyun Kyung is a Korean theologian. Her book *Struggle
to Be the Sun Again* is a strong statement of Asian women's theology. According to Chung, theology is recorded in the hearts of
many women. Chung writes:

> Theology must become democratized. Since all conscious ex-
> perience is already interpreted experience, Asian women's
> experience of the divine already has its own theological inter-
> pretation.... Asian women's theology is *live-ing* theology....
> It is living liberation and wholeness here and now.... Asian
> women's theology...is also their vision quest....For Asian
> women, theology is a language of hope, dreams and poetry.[21]

Because of this grounding of theological explorations among the
people rather than in the confines of the academy, Chung notes
that theologians' roles must shift to genuinely living out the "radical egalitarian values of Jesus Christ," being one with poor women
and always conscious of their shared cultural grounding. The importance of culture, the centering of theological work in the place
of everyday people, is critical for theologians working with people
other than the dominant classes. The note of culture surfaces in
each of these theologians' works.

Noel Leo Erskine is an Afro-Caribbean theologian who aims
to discuss theology in a way that reflects the lives of Caribbean
peoples. Because of the development of black theology in the
United States and of African theology, Caribbean peoples' religious
realities were often overlooked. Erskine seeks to "decolonize" the-

ology from the Western European traditions as well as from the dominance of U.S. black theologies.

In his book *Decolonizing Theology,* Erskine surveyed many definitions of theology by African scholars that highlight tensions between their cultural realities and those of the West. "What then is African theology? John Mbiti speaks of it as 'an understanding of the Faith according to the total situation of our peoples — historical, cultural, contemporary and anticipated or possible future.' Idowu refers to African theology as 'Faith-in-self-expression.' "[22] From this overview, Erskine reaches some important conclusions.

The first is obvious: all black people cannot be forced into a single category. Particular situations must be taken into account. Therefore, theological statements must be grounded in the context of *this* people, in *this* time. Second, Erskine's explorations raised up connections between different black groups with shared histories of oppression and different cultural backgrounds. Culture is an important consideration for liberation theologies, which will be discussed later in this chapter.

Black theologians in the United States are indebted to James Cone, whose 1969 work, *Black Theology and Black Power,*[23] began a dialogue that has grown over the years. As two recent examples, Josiah Young and Garth Kasimu Baker-Fletcher offer different views of theologies' tasks. Josiah Young developed a view of black theology called "Pan-African."[24] Young attempts to synthesize divergent views of African people in the diaspora and to find connections. He draws especially from W. E. B. Du Bois's and Marcus Garvey's ideas of Pan-Africanism. Young includes theologies from the United States, Africa, and Europe, asserting that the central task for Pan-African theology is to assist black people to resist oppression and create new cultures. For Young, a Pan-African theology is not necessarily Christian or Muslim or from any other faith tradition but has an ecumenical component of the commonalities among black people: "African descent, cultural modalities, and, especially among the poor, radical similarity in socioeconomic suffering."[25] Interestingly, Young's 1992 overview of black theologies around the world included no black women. This glaring fact sets into relief that black women's voices have been too often excluded from black theologies. This theme of exclusion by black men will surface in later discussions within womanist theology.

Contrasted with Young's work, Garth Kasimu Baker-Fletcher's *Xodus: An African American Male Journey*[26] offered a more inclusive theological agenda. The tasks for theology in this agenda are for men to genuinely listen to women; to utilize language and black culture in stating religious meaning; and to partner with black women for the good of all people.

James Cone is considered a founder of black theological dialogue and continues its development. He has presented challenges to Christian theology by taking both black and white theologians to task for the work of not addressing the racism embedded in Christianity:

> White theologians in seminaries, university departments of religion and divinity schools, and professional societies refused to acknowledge white supremacy as a theological problem and continued their business as usual, as if the lived experience of blacks was theologically vacuous. One reason black theologians have not developed an enduring race critique stems from their uncritical identification with the dominant Christian and integrationist tradition in African American history.[27]

From these discussions, some defining features of Christian liberation theologies can be drawn:

- Liberation theologies are not merely academic, but connected with people's lives. Everything from history to current political realities becomes a focus for theological reflection.

- Culture is celebrated, not ignored, and is seen as central to human understandings. Being human in community becomes a doorway to know God in ever new ways.

- The humanness of Jesus is understood as being in relationship with people of color, in light of shared oppression and sorrow. This way of knowing Jesus inspired the spirituals of enslaved Africans.

- Christian faith is to be lived: it is not an activity for the weak but strengthens commitment for justice and love. In particular, relationships with the poor and oppressed are significant measures of lived faith.

- Theologians therefore use analysis to connect faith-practice with faith-theory in order to invite people to deeper faith and construct theologies that reflect these realities.

Of all the general features of liberation theologies, culture is a critically important aspect of being human. Cultural analysis has significantly shifted paradigms of theology.

Culture and Theology

North Atlantic theological constructions had, in previous developments, aimed to name aspects universal to all people. The universal was understood as the objective idea that was true for all groups: objective because it was developed beyond race or culture or any other human subjectivity. But it is arrogant to believe that finite humans can achieve such a goal, for all humans are mired in social frameworks. A specific culture's realities build the edges of the framework. Culture is complex in the ways it is woven through life as both a thing and a process.

African American culture has been uniquely developed. Sidney Mintz and Richard Price posit the idea that African "cognitive orientations" were part of the mind-sets of the enslaved Africans. With this concept, they define how African American cultures developed and were maintained in black communities. These remnants continue to have some life in black American communities, often without a specific one-to-one correspondence in any African culture. The existence of these remnants gives credence to the theories of Mintz and Price, who define African cognitive orientations as

> On the one hand, basic assumptions about social relations (which values motivate individuals, how one deals with others in social situations, and matters of interpersonal style), and, on

the other, basic assumptions and expectations about the way the world functions phenomenologically (for instance, beliefs about causality, and how particular causes are revealed). We would argue that certain common orientations to reality may tend to focus the attention of individuals from West and Central African cultures upon similar kinds of events, even though the ways for handling these events may seem quite diverse in formal terms.[28]

This web of relationships between African American and African conceptualizations can be pointed out in a variety of places. For example, the historian Albert Raboteau concisely states the African understandings of the interconnections of person, community, and nature: "Africans conceived of the individual self . . . as constituted by a web of kinship relations. . . . In this traditional worldview, aspects of life and nature that moderns view as impersonal were seen as personal and relational."[29] These ideas were part of the "cognitive orientations" brought by the enslaved Africans to the New World. They became part of the active resistance against dehumanizing definitions: "Folk beliefs [too] provided hope, assurance, and a sense of group identification, but they had another dimension as well: they actually offered slaves sources of power and knowledge alternative to those existing within the world of the master class."[30] These are complex ways to think about culture, made richer when the importance of location is considered.

Culture is a shifting panorama, changing across place as well. The black cultural expressions in Chicago, Illinois, are not the same as those in Baton Rouge, Louisiana. Geechee, Creole, third-generation Jamaican, or black Cherokee bring different customs to the black conversational table. Specific traditions and material artifacts reveal the differing cultural realities. As a Yoruba proverb states: the norm in this family is a taboo elsewhere.

Research becomes complicated when considering histories, specific regions, or African connections. Another factor to examine is the resource pool for information on African American people. Limited written and material documentation from the perspective of black people is a painful reminder of a history of oppression. Past research on black people was often skewed by embedded

stereotypical views. Labels like "culturally deprived" have been applied to African Americans as late as the 1980s. Often, scholars
have first had to locate resources before they could begin to develop theories. Tools for constructing a theology that takes culture
into account might include folktales, stories, or literature. In black
theology, the everyday realities of black people's lives become an
important basis for construction. This approach requires a willingness to utilize a variety of sources as well as listen to stories of past
and present.

These cultural perspectives of sources and histories should not
be used uncritically or they could result in the creation of romantic,
nostalgic theories. Sociocritical analysis undertakes another level
of deconstruction and considers the origins, the sociology, and
the underlying philosophies of the present moment's cultural constructions. For liberation theologians, this work will specifically
incorporate race, class, gender, and other categories of oppression
as critical lenses. There are many methodologies drawn from other
disciplines that may be used in constructing liberation theologies.
History, ethnography, literary criticism, political science, economics, law, and anthropology all have useful methods that may be
needed in theological development.

Among African American women, there is diversity that must be
addressed in some fashion in order to avoid reducing the realities
of black women to simplistic categories. Marcia Riggs is a womanist ethicist who mines the historical writings of black women,
grounding womanist scholarship across time, culture, and region.
Her *Can I Get a Witness? Prophetic Religious Voices of African
American Women* begins with an excerpt from the autobiography
of a woman named Elizabeth, an eighteenth-century slave, and
ends with the words of twentieth-century Congresswoman Shirley
Chisholm. Riggs states that her location of primary texts by black
women that narrowly focuses on the prophetic religious tradition is "a work of reconstruction and retrieval, [which] seeks to
document that tradition as predecessor to the current womanist
religious scholarship."[31] This range of black women across time
and life situations demonstrates connections in spite of condition or region. In each case, the women analyzed some aspect of
society in personal and religious terms. Riggs notes three com-

monly held themes throughout the women's words: the personal, intercommunal, and intracommunal dimensions. African American women have been far from passive in the face of constructions of race, gender, and class, and their words in the primary texts powerfully confirm their responses. Riggs's work demonstrates how cultural and regional diversity is flattened by experiences of oppression. Womanist theology participates, in this point in time, in that historically grounded critique of abusive power. As will be seen, womanist theology fully participates in liberative analysis, while constructing prophetic visions.

Discussion Questions

1. Can you identify some aspect or event of your own cultural background that has an accompanying religious expression? Examples include holiday celebrations, home altars, funeral rituals, and so on.

2. How do you define an educated person? What do you think is important in a college education? Why?

3. How do you view the human body? Does your cultural background shape your view? How does your religious thinking shape your view of the body?

4. Define wisdom. Where and how can a person get it?

5. Identify your commitments as a scholar.

Chapter 3

Womanist Theology

Womanist approaches to theology aim to develop a variety of theological constructions in which black women are the main subject. Where is God in the lives of African American women? How do black women name God? Like liberation theologies discussed in the previous chapter, womanist theology is a place of discovery, in faith, that analyzes both politics and culture.

Although it must be analytical, womanist theology is also recorded in the hearts of black women and bears a strong resemblance to jazz. It uses many instruments, works within a different rhythmic structure, and depends upon the creativity and skill of individual artists. Jazz utilizes improvisation, which is ordering the never-before-voiced. Such improvisation requires a demanding level of skill and the ability to move free of the written music. Womanist theology also demands skill, a movement in the light of faith from the Western written page to a statement of the seldom-voiced experience of African American women. Womanist theology, then, critically draws from the many meanings of faith in the lives of black women in order to assess doctrinal and ecclesial constructions and to begin reconstructions that have relevance, meaning, and power in their lives.

"Ordinary" Theologies

I think spirituality has to do with my faith, my beliefs and my stewardship.... And I believe that is part of what drives me.... I guess a few years ago I might not have thought much about it, but now it's very important. Not religion... so spirituality for me is a culmination of everything that I do and its

46

impact.... It's all right for women to celebrate, validate, and educate.... Part of our [Black Women's Health Project] spirituality is the whole comfort zone we offer to black women. You know, without selling out... There's something we offer that's different. We call it "the magic." You know, we do our magic and how do you explain magic? You want to call it mystical or something but we say that spirituality is really part of the foundation of what we are. Where sisters can come together and be comfortable. And all types of sisters.[1]

The above words are from a woman named Azana and indicate the rich heritage of spirituality operating in black communities, taking particular shapes for African American women. Azana's words are applicable to womanist theology with an imperative to begin with black women's lives as texts, celebrating and validating their own selves.

The concept of lives as "texts" has entered into scholarship through literary criticism and historiography. Documents which have developed historically cannot necessarily be applied to people today. The structures that worked in the past may not be sufficient for addressing contemporary dilemmas of genetic engineering, technological divides, or globalization. The texts of lives yield information that mere statistics cannot; most people are aware that numbers can be made to lie, depending on the person who interprets them. Viewed as texts, human lives also require interpretation. At the same time, human lives stand in interpretation of their times: Who are the powerful or the marginalized and why? Interpretations of individual or communal lives, church doctrine, or scripture from the perspectives of people of color have provided a critical difference in the development of liberation theologies.

Azana's words indicate a difference in perspective: the place where black women begin religious explorations is in daily life, not in exercises in theory or doctrine. African American women have rich traditions of faith meanings that inform their lives. These are ordinary theologies that respond to life situations. Sometimes mistaken as superstition or dismissed as having no value, these theologies spring from the values that life has taught black women. This is the spirituality, or the magic, to which Azana refers. The idea of ordinary theologies echoes Philomena Essed's naming of the "everyday racisms" black women experience.[2] Essed's study encompassed black women in the United States and Britain. She found that the everyday experiences of racism were often insidious, subtle, debilitating, and served as preparation for bigger racist incidents. Ordinary theologies, which are culturally derived, ubiquitous, and effective in creating new realities for black women, are empowering in overcoming everyday racisms as well as major events in racism or discrimination.

These ordinary theologies are expressed in many ways. They are not merely intellectualized concepts, but are deeply felt and involve women's daily practices. Practices with religious meanings may come from the tradition of organized religions, but those referred to here are from women's folkways. Two of these religious practices that often surface among black women describe their capacity to empower.

One such practice is that of "going to the water" as a place of prayer and meditation. Some black women report that places (not necessarily churches) are able to assist them in focusing their prayer lives. They seek such places where there is a sense of safety and power and spirituality. Water, which is one of these "places," has great significance in West African traditional religions and also has lingering meanings that for some black women in the United States connect with themes of "old-time" religion, a connection that has yet to be fully explored. A second practice of some black women is "reading signs." Signs are often in nature: certain birds or sunlight's appearance at a certain moment can be interpreted as visible communication from God. (There is further discussion of African traditional religions as a source of religious knowledge for womanist theology in chapter 7.)

Black women often report some sense of interactive prayer. One woman might say: "I took my problem to the Lord, and left it there," with another black woman's response: "Don't pick it up again." God is understood as a partner in life rather than a distant observer. Black women report experiencing a sense of openness to God's guidance: they expect a response, whether in the form of a sign or a problem resolved. Prayer is understood as powerful. Such approaches to the sacred occur often in the lives of black women.

At the core of these ordinary theologies is faith. Faith, for black women, becomes a self-defining center that resists socially constructed stereotypes. "God is able" is both a battle cry and a statement of faith. The development of black women's faith is not merely a response to social conditions and is not a form of denial. Faith can provide the alternative space in which black women become self-empowered. Faith in this framework has the cultural groundings of the black community and black women's networks, but it involves a lifelong process of spiritual maturation. The deep belief patterns are not always connected to a specific church community; it is not unusual for black women to tell of their spiritual journeys away from organized religion. "Baby, they're trying to take my joy," an elderly black woman reported as she withdrew her membership from a church community. These understandings of faith become central in womanist theological reflections.

Womanist theology must draw from the meanings that already exist in black women's lives. The lived theologies of individual black women cannot be dismissed as the empty activities of the ignorant. Womanist theologians recognize the richness of black women's communal expressions of theology. These lived theologies become part of the womanist theological text.

Communal Dimensions

Black women's spiritual and religious understandings are culturally transmitted. Black women usually do not have to leave home and search for the concepts mentioned above: mothers take their daughters to the water, and grandmothers explain the meanings of the signs. This implies a communal dimension or socialization process into these ways of religious thinking.

Darlene Clark Hine, in her research as a historian, wrote of her discovery of this communal dimension of black women's work:

> "Making community" means the processes of creating religious, educational, health care, philanthropic, political, and familial institutions and professional organizations that enabled our people to survive.... Black women created essential

new communities and erected vast female networks during
the transitions from slavery to freedom, from farm to city.
It was through "making community" that Black women
were able to redefine themselves, project sexual respectability,
reshape morality, and define a new aesthetic.[3]

The historical familial structures were broader in black communities than the nuclear family of father, mother, and children.
Kinship was determined differently, becoming a matter of physical and emotional survival for black people. Networks were built
that crossed birth family lines. Anthropologists refer to this pattern
of building family ties among unrelated persons as "fictive" kin.
An example of a developed role/relationship in black communities
that operated beyond birth family lines is that of the wisdom-
sharing caregiver, usually an older woman, sometimes called the
"othermother."

Mothering is a critical role in black communities for transmission of folkways and wisdom. With the Emancipation Proclama-
tion, the role of mothers in African American homes was shaped by
new realities as well as the need for personal and community survival in a still-hostile world. In 1905, in *The Voice of the Negro*,
Josephine Bruce wrote:

> The Negro home is rapidly assuming the position designated
> for it. It is distinctly becoming the center of social and intel-
> lectual life; it is building up strength and righteousness in its
> sons and daughters, equipping them for the inevitable battles
> of life.[4]

This self-righteous note was sounded repeatedly by black women
who, for the survival of the black community, used churchwomen's
movements to lift their people and help them climb away from
the remnants of slavery and toward full participation in American
life.[5] Historian Evelyn Brooks Higginbotham has researched black
churchwomen in the nineteenth century,[6] considering specific ways
in which Northern white and Southern black Baptist churches were
conduits for the education of black women into acceptable (read
white, middle-class) home-life patterns, a process that employed
magazines, letters, and educational programs. Motherhood, de-

fined this way, would have emulated that of white women. Despite such attempts at cultural programming, black life in America could not become a mirror of the dominant white culture.

African American women were able to expand their understandings of mothering to meet their needs. Patricia Hill Collins refers to motherhood in the black communities as an institution in itself. "Motherhood can serve as a site where Black women express and learn the power of self-definition, the importance of valuing and respecting ourselves, the necessity of self-reliance and independence, and a belief in Black women's empowerment."[7] Drawing from African cognitive frameworks, mothering included both birth mothers and the "othermothers" of the communities. One result of this concept of mothering is "organized, resilient, women-centered networks of bloodmothers and othermothers."[8] These networks were the cultural groundings in the development of the nineteenth- and twentieth-century women's club movement, as well as other activist efforts by black women.

The black women's institution of motherhood, particularly the communal "othermother" aspect, also serves a healing function, underlining values held dearly by black women. Carol Boyce Davies drew from literature by black women to discuss the healing aspects of mothering:

> Mothering and healing are intricately connected and of central thematic importance.... Reflecting a distinctly Black feminist point of view, these writers reveal that Black women, at certain junctures in their lives, require healing and renewal and that Black women themselves have to become the healers/mothers for each other when there is such a need.... [The writers also communicate] the important message that survival alone and persistent mothering of others cannot be considered sufficient.[9]

Such mothering among black women is reciprocal, emphasizing women's responsibilities and possibilities. "Significantly, much of this mothering is directed at releasing the inner self being suffocated by race and sex oppression."[10] Mothering functions to fashion networks of women who contribute significantly to the creation of black identities and communities.

Toinette M. Eugene looks to black women's proverbs, which she calls the "Mama saids," as a location for this wisdom source:[11]

> A tremendously significant source of our cultural and religious heritage has been preserved and transmitted to us in what may be called a litany of "Mama Saids..." Mama said: "God don't like ugly!" *So mystical!*...Mama said: "Don't you listen to anything bad that people say about you — you may be poor, you may be slow, or struggling to make it, but you're somebody special, baby. You're God's own child, and that's what counts." *Regardless.*[12]

As in mothering, black women extended nurturing through the construction of formal and informal networks, of which the women's club movement was one element. African American women's ability to network can become extremely positive as a source for developing personal and communal resources beyond merely surviving. Formal or informal networking continues among black women to this day. The Detroit Metropolitan Black Women's Health Project is an exemplary model of the ways activism is enacted through a network of women. The project, a chapter of a national project, promotes wellness among African American women through grassroots, communal efforts. Azana, whose words reflected an ordinary theology, is a member of this project. Her words indicate the relationship of project members to other black women: centered on promoting total wellness, advocating, caring, hoping to nurture, and inviting participation. Frances is another member of the project who explained the sacred space that black women create through their networking:

> The key elements...are safety, security and opportunity. Demonstrate that we can create community anywhere. Women often say, "This is the first time I've been able to talk about myself and have someone really listen." A woman gets to focus on herself, to experience acceptance by a number of folks and to increase her own self-esteem and power.[13]

Creating a sacred space is one of the most important aspects of the project. At one meeting, a member read a poem directed toward other black women who are not involved in the

project. "We're going to care-nap you," she said at a conference, which elicited nods and smiles from those in attendance.
Reaching out to other black women was viewed as liberative for
all women involved. "Sister-power" is generated, which results in
self-empowerment:

> I think what we [the project] offer women when they get in-
> volved is an opportunity to just share what's going on in their
> life.... Because we don't take time for ourselves, the mere
> fact that you can be around some other black women and
> share what's going on in your life is a big help. And the other
> part is sisterhood, and my concept of sisterhood is a group
> of women being able to work together around a project. And
> there's a benefit in that. When you work together, you kind of
> learn about each other and that comes from our old activist
> days, you know, the best kind of struggle is when people are
> doing it together.... See, when sisters are worried about how
> I'm gonna feed my kids, how I'm going to get to work, to pay
> my light bill, it's a little difficult to be thinking about I got
> all this power. But I do think that power comes from within
> the group — I know that's what helped me evolve. I know
> that there's a group of powerful women out here. I can pick
> up the phone and I can call. It doesn't mean they got any
> money, but when we come together, it's almost like we got
> something spiritual, something magical about that. It's also
> made me kind of fearless.[14]

The self-empowerment of the women through discovering and
expressing their own needs and the consequent empowerment of
the wider community were expected outcomes of involvement in
the group. Power was a freely discussed issue in meetings because
it was considered intimately related to health. Power — whether at
home, school, or work — is a life issue that black women discuss
in self-help groups related to spirituality.

In spite of such communal networking, contradictions and dissonances among African American women still rise, as discussions
in the first chapter indicated. Because of the oppression of gender
entrapment, black women sometimes suffer a lack of self-esteem
and feel unloved. The need to survive has also created the need

for many black women to develop personal strength, which can also lead to damaging personal relationships. These conflicting personal/communal dimensions will surface in myriad ways in the constructions of womanist theology.

African American women construct religious identities from all these sources: grassroots organizing; mothering/nurturance; familial values; and community networking and activism. All these culturally grounded sources are informed by the critically important institution of black religious life termed "the black church."[15]

Black people have a history of finding strength in their communal religious lives. Church life has been a center of information, education, social support, and cultural transmission.[16] While some theorists claim that religion is an opiate of the oppressed, many African Americans have found ways to utilize religion as a personal and communal center of subversive action. Howard Thurman, considered the forefather of many contemporary black theologians, wrote in a 1947 essay:

> [Religious faith] taught a people how to ride high to life, to look squarely in the face of those that argue most dramatically against all hope. . . . With untutored hands — with a sure artistry and genius created out of a vast vitality, a concept of God was wrenched from the Sacred Book, the Bible, the chronicle of a people who had learned through great necessity the secret meaning of suffering. This total experience enabled them to reject annihilation and affirm a terrible right to live.[17]

Faith and prayer in black communities have formed creative, contrary people who take religion seriously. Religious expression takes multiple forms, from music to new denominations. African American women have participated in the lives of churches, creating something of their own identities in the process. Cheryl Townsend Gilkes's important text *If It Wasn't for the Women*[18] presents a historically grounded view of black women's contributions to the constructions of the black church. Using sources from black church records to African cognitive orientations, Gilkes demonstrates that black women's creativity in constructing identities in religious and social life is time-honored in African American communities.

Martha Jean "the Queen" Steinberg was a Detroit radio personality and preacher who died in 1999. She liberally dispensed advice on her radio program through the 1960s and 1970s, seeking to empower black women.[19] By the 1980s, she had founded a church, with its ministries performed by the "Queen's Workers." There are hundreds of Queens across the country, black women who redefine religious possibilities for themselves and other women.

Beyond the ordinary theologies of black women's lives, formed by the historical connections that Gilkes points out, and grounded in faith, the religious activism of the Queens becomes more defining of theological constructions. Womanist theology is informed and inspired by traditions of black women working with religious thought in new ways.

Constructing Womanist Theology

Alice Walker is a writer and activist who coined the term "womanist" in her book *In Search of Our Mothers' Gardens,* presenting the definition in four parts.[20] She subverts the dry details of the standard idea of a dictionary-type definition by crafting poetry to convey her meaning. The definition incorporates the language rhythms and meanings of black women. Walker states that the word "womanist" is a derivation of "womanish, ... from the black folk expression, 'You acting womanish.' " Walker includes the historical and communal dimensions of black women, indicating a history of women leading the enslaved to freedom, and stating that a womanist is "committed to survival and wholeness of entire people, male and female." The sexuality of black women takes a central place in the definition, women loving women or men, "sexually and/or nonsexually." Walker captures the holistic way that black women embrace diversity, within self and others, in one of the most lyrical sections of the definition. "Loves the Spirit. Loves love and food and roundness. Loves struggle."[21] Walker's words become a conduit for expression of what it means for black women to be women. Walker's definition is powerful, gathering components of black women's lives in order to define what feminism means to them.

Many black women saw the construction of feminism as ir-
relevant in their lives. White feminists, who only minimally ac-
knowledged the impact of race and class, marginalized black
women's needs and realities. The divide between black and white
American women had roots in the suffragist movement of the
nineteenth century. In 1986, Barbara Hilkert Andolsen, a white
feminist, painstakingly traced the history of racism within feminism's growth.[22] Following the Civil War, as the push for women's
suffrage grew, the white women leading the movement determined
that the exclusion of black women was politically advantageous
in order to prove to white men and Southern women the serious-
ness of the cause. Certainly there were black women pushing for
the vote as well, but the very visible division of black and white
women was another missed opportunity in American history for
collaboration among those who are oppressed. Toinette Eugene, a
womanist ethicist, states:

> Within this historical framework of past and present hostility
> black women have always perceived networks of relational-
> ity in the liberation struggle differently from white women.
> Domesticity has never been seen as entirely oppressive but
> rather as a vehicle for building family life under slavery; male/
> female relationships have always been more egalitarian; there
> has been less emphasis on women's work as different from
> and inferior to men's.... It is easy to understand why many
> black people today see the white feminist movement as an
> attempt to divide black people.[23]

The definition of "womanist" became a pivotal concept among
black women religious scholars. Katie Cannon reflects that the
term for her personally was "philosophically medicinal." For black
scholars of religion, especially black women connected with the
American Academy of Religion, Cannon names the concept a
"benchmark event":

> The chief function of womanism is not merely to replace
> one set of elitist, hegemonic texts...with another set of
> Afrocentric texts....Rather our objective is to use Walker's
> four part definition as a critical, methodological framework

for challenging inherited traditions for their collusion with androcentric patriarchy as well as a catalyst in overcoming oppressive situations through revolutionary acts of rebellion.[24]

These acts of rebellion included the construction of womanist theology and other acts of liberation. Womanist theology begins in ethical analysis. With ethics, black women can place their lives in a reflective theological context.

The first chapter surfaced a variety of issues that African American women face in daily life. Many of these issues have been socially constructed as "normal" in America because the usual ordering of mainstream society is white, middle-class, middle-aged, male, heterosexual, and able-bodied. Black women are invisible and excluded because they can never fit all these social constrictions. One of the members of the Black Women's Health Project, Lisa, referred to the omission of African American women from this schema: "Our health and well-being is not part of what this system looks at . . . because we're not white, because we're not rich and male, because they can't deal with us."[25] Instead, she states that black women need to come to new understandings:

You know, everything is for the children, the family. Well, it's time to stop that . . . and claim the power that is ours. A wonderful dead mother isn't doing her children any good. . . . We have been living a contradiction. I think we've always, since we've been in this country, realized how strong we are, how powerful we are — at the same time we live in a culture that wants to make damn sure that we don't forget we're not.[26]

This contradictory living informs and forms black women's thoughts. An ethical response is needed to race *and* class *and* gender *and* all other forms of oppressions. African American women do not have the luxury to pick and choose, for we are bombarded with multiplying oppressions. This multiplication of injustices moves womanist ethicists into specific directions in order to address these problems: there can be no hierarchy of oppres-

sions, no addressing one and ignoring the other, if there is ever to
be real justice.

Ethics can be defined, in a much-shortened way, as an analysis of life. The determination of right or wrong, good or bad,
depends on the moral values a community brings to the analytical process. Ethical dilemmas exist all around us, from the type
of work we do, to how we raise our children, to how we spend
our money, to how we vote. Ethics does not merely consider problems we encounter but begins to frame the basis by which we
ought to make judgments and act. Ethics, from a liberatory stance,
considers power relationships in society, deconstructs oppressions,
and provides new paradigms for thinking about "the way things
always are."

Womanist theology must be grounded by womanist ethics. Such
grounding is dearly bought because it is based on the complexities
of lived experience. To begin womanist theology in some heavenly
place and then come back to the human will not effectively speak
to the religious and practical realities of black women. It will not
work because to do so would deny the holiness of black women's
lives, lives that others have attempted to define and erase. The very
concept of God becomes problematic if black women are denied
a sense of self. Instead, experiences can become a precious portal
for theological reflection. This ethics-first approach to womanist
theology, based on the texts of African American women's lives,
analyzes reflections on life experiences. It also yields a description
of the values that black women hold important in life. If these values do not conform with those of America's dominant society, then
black women will use alternative bases for decision making.

An ethnographic study by Dorothy Pennington provides an
illustration of black women's decision processes.[27] The women interviewed by Pennington experienced their work as an extension of
self and a source of validation. Resisting narrow definitions, they
found ways to expand beyond boundaries. For those in the study,
this extension involved quitting particular workplaces and sometimes starting new, very experimental business ventures. Several of
the women in the study had advanced degrees but departed from
business-school-solid career paths. In each case, God or the universe was the motivation and the encouragement to take the step.

In other words, the religious context was not viewed as separate from the social, and the professional was not divorced from the personal. A relationship with God was somehow in active conversation with life decisions. Such forms of decision making would seem ludicrous to some who might not share the value system that informed these women's lives.

Katie Cannon speaks of the task of the womanist religious scholar as that of analysis of black women's movement from death to life. Drawing lessons from history,

> we investigate contestable issues according to official records, which seldom offer any indication why things have gone wrong nor why benefactors of oppression strive to maintain certain principles.... Womanist religious scholars insist that individuals look back at race, sex, and class constructions before it is too late and put forth critical analysis in such a way that the errors of the past will not be repeated.[28]

In other words, womanist ethical analysis expects the outcome of ethical action.

With ethics as the point of entry, womanist theology begins processes of moving toward theological theories, in which hermeneutics is a component. Hermeneutics is, generally, the science of interpretation and is based on a variety of factors, including social institutions, values, traditions, language, ritual, history, statistics, and, for people of faith, sacred scriptures. Hermeneutics for theological scholars is often applied to scriptural studies, thereby limiting the idea of interpretation to a written text. However, the science of interpretation crosses into all areas of life. When black women listen to presidential debates or encounter the police officer on the street, different tapes run through their minds than run through those of white members of American society. Certainly, black women's understanding of themselves differs from that held by the dominant culture. This is not new. Offering an oral history of the formerly enslaved, Ann Parker related her experiences under enslavement. At the age of 103, she remembered, "I ain't had no daddy, 'cause queens don't marry, and my mammy, Junny, was a queen in Africa. They kidnaps her and steals her away from her throne.... Yes, she was a queen, and when she told them niggers that she was, they bowed down to her. She told them not to tell it."[29] This indicates a different understanding of the meaning of relationships and importance, on the part of mother, daughter, and community. Ann Parker's hermeneutics, shared with her community, will yield a negative view of the enslavers and a positive view of herself and her mother, the queen.

Ordinary theologies, ethical analyses, and hermeneutics are some of the basic tools for constructing womanist theology.

Defining Womanist Theology

Womanist theology becomes a center where all the ideas already raised have a home with safe space for discussion and discovery. Womanist theology is an opportunity to state the meanings of God in the real time of black women's lives. Womanist theology explores the magic of black women's religious meaning-worlds, in all the various forms. Historical and cultural realities, from black women's perspectives, also need expression in theological terms. Womanist theology brings unstated assumptions about black women to a place where they can be explored, refined, and celebrated or debunked.

Delores Williams intensely explored theological frameworks of womanist "God-talk" in *Sisters in the Wilderness*. She states defining features of womanist theology:

> Womanist theology attempts to help black women see, affirm and have confidence in the importance of their experience and faith for determining the character of the Christian religion in the African-American community. Womanist theology challenges all oppressive forces impeding black women's struggle for survival and for the development of a positive, productive quality of life conducive to women's and the family's freedom and well-being. Womanist theology opposes all oppression based on race, sex, class, sexual preference, physical disability and caste.... Womanist theology... also branches off in its own direction, introducing new issues and constructing new analytical categories.[30]

Womanist theology has been under construction since the mid-1980s. Womanist theologians understand that the theological enterprise is in response to black women's living conditions. One challenge for womanist theology is to record African American women's religious meanings. Black women have been overlooked and misrepresented in other areas of life, but this is even more the case in the area of religious meanings. Here, black women's religious realities have often been relegated to the sphere of superstition: the image of the evil black voodoo priestess is the stuff of B-grade movies. If black women's lives and religious meanings have been deemed unworthy of serious study, then womanist theologians must employ the interdisciplinary tools of history, ethnography, literary criticism, folklore, sociology, economics, and medicine. Uses of different disciplines are liberatory practices. The rich textures and gifts of African American religious lives, from women's perspectives, need exploration.

One issue of contention about these constructions is that of relationships: To what degree should womanists explain themselves or their ideas to existing Western traditions? Katie Cannon draws from her encounters with white scholars who deem African American women "nonpolitical":

> I asked one gentleman . . . what he meant by saying that womanists are apolitical. Not even sighing or missing a heartbeat, he responded, "Well, it seems to me that womanist work is not talking about White people." I said that is correct. We do not begin nor end our work with White people on our eyeballs. So he and others conclude that if Euro-Americans are not the focal point of departure then womanist work is without political significance.[31]

Use of interdisciplinary tools is important in setting new directions for the construction of womanist theology. Equally important, as indicated by the Cannon quote, is the necessity that womanists set the direction from their own unique perspectives. Womanist theology is not an apology for the existence of black women. Genuine dialogue and collaboration with other theological traditions can only occur when the statements of womanist theology are honestly developed. Such development mirrors the growth seen in other liberation theologies, with which womanist theologians have begun to build alliances.

Womanist theology is not merely about building political alliances. An important task of womanist theology is to reconsider Christian doctrine with black women's lives as the point of departure. Considering the issue of christology, Delores Williams turns to womanist questions of doctrine:

> Is the subject of the christological inquiry, that is, the meaning of the person of Jesus, broad enough or relevant enough to serve as an analytical tool for assessing *all* the African-American Christian understanding of Jesus or God? ... What are the appropriate tools for exploring the meaning of Jesus in an Afrocentric American context?[32]

From these questions, she posits a need for doctrine that "emerges from African-American people's experience with God," in order to name the works of God among black people as well as the fully human responses that are part of the Christian heritage and memory. Williams challenges womanist theologians to

> begin raising questions about the analytical appropriateness of *all* traditional doctrinal categories for interrogating African-American women's experience — questions that trouble the theological waters.... Our purpose is not to trouble the waters just for the sake of raising a fuss. *Our purpose is to present more precisely what African-American women and the African-American community have and do believe and to exercise a prophetic womanist theological task in relation to this belief.*[33]

The womanist theological task has been developing over the last years; it is prophetic and calls for a more holistic approach to the purposes and processes of black communal life.

Two areas of black religious community life are relevant to womanist theology's development. One area is analysis of and work with black male theologians. How do their constructions view black women? The other area is that of relationships with and within church communities. How have churches treated black women in pastoral practice? Each of these will be considered in much more detail in chapter 5.

The challenges of considering the religious lives of black women within formal programs are immense and often daunting. "Is this work legitimately theological?" some scholars ask. Such a question implies a deep racism and sexism that degrade the religious lives of black women. Katie Cannon writes powerfully of the isolation of black women in seminary settings:

> As Black women pursuing advanced theological degrees, alienation, isolation, and marginalization were our daily fare. Even with the requisite credentials for matriculation in hand, we were constantly barraged with arrogance and insults, suspicion and insensitivity, backhand compliments and tongue-in-cheek naiveté. The worlds of divinity school, denominational headquarters, regional judicatory offices, and local parishes, between which we negotiated, demanded different and often wrenching allegiances. But we continued to study.[34]

It may be helpful before proceeding to delineate some of the key points of womanist theology that have been raised so far:

- Womanist theology uncovers and incorporates the ordinary theologies of black women's lives.

- The communal dimension of black women's experiences includes the values of social activism and the creation of safe spaces. This communal dimension extends into the methodology of womanist theology itself, where theologians and ethicists collaborate rather than compete.

- Alice Walker's definition sets important parameters of discovery and implies a methodology that is interdisciplinary while remaining centered on all aspects of black women's lives.

- Ethics becomes a starting point from which to build a womanist theology, particularly in its continuing critical social analysis.

- Ongoing dialogue and openness are essential, particularly because womanist theology breaks with some of the dynamics of Western theological construction. This dialogic dimension is seen particularly in connection with other liberative theologies, particularly black and feminist, for which womanist theology is corrective.

These general ideas will assist in the next chapters' discussions. Not intended to be exhaustive, these principles set some parameters for further exploration of womanist theology.

Discussion Questions

1. Give an example of African American women's "invisibility." Do other women in U.S. society experience something similar? Do men?

2. Identify one story from the newspaper in which black women are the subjects. How are they written about? Are there unstated assumptions about black women? Are ethical issues indicated?

3. What is the importance of personal and communal experiences in constructing theology?

4. Define womanist theology. Why is ethics the first step in its construction?

Part II

The first three chapters assisted in laying groundwork for under-standing the context of womanist theology. The first chapter discussed the sociocultural framework that informs African American women's worlds. The second chapter turned to the dynamics of theology itself, in the Western and in the liberation traditions. The third chapter gave a basic definition of womanist theology. These underpinnings provide the ground for the next pages.

An important aspect of the development of womanist theology is often unstated: black women are not primarily focused on addressing the concerns of white theologians. Instead, African American women address the concerns of their lives from their own perspectives. This is not insulating but liberating as black women create public venues in which to explore the realities of their intellectual and spiritual lives. Some of the tensions, problems, and rewards of such explorations will inform the following pages.

Chapter 4

Womanist Constructions

An exploration of womanist constructions begins with careful deliberation on some of the earliest full texts. These texts laid down the arguments and focus areas while setting several directions. These works cannot be separated from the authors' growth as scholars and leaders. These developments owe much to parallel developments in other disciplines and along sociopolitical fronts.

The 1970s were a fertile time in which many people began to state their own realities. Black women were participants and leaders in these statements. Angela Davis was a political prisoner whose Marxist ideas indicated new global realities in which other black women could participate. Writer Audre Lorde set up new challenges to white feminists and began new analyses of black women's sexuality. June Jordan's poetry and political activism uncovered new avenues for black women to think of their own possibilities. Mary Helen Washington's literary scholarship began the work of excavating African American historical women's writings. The discovery of a legacy of words and wisdom from the pens of ancestral black women inspired many others. This work of retrieval and restatement informed religious scholarship also. James Cone began that retrieval and restatement process for the development of black theology. Womanist religious scholarship began with essays from Delores Williams and Toinette Eugene, among others. Conversations occurring among black women religion scholars furthered the development of their ideas. With the publication of several full-length texts in the 1980s, womanist theology began.

Signal Texts

Three critically important texts published in the 1980s are noted
for their contributions to the development of womanist thought.
Of the three, two works were revised from doctoral dissertations,
and the other book resulted from pastoral work and theological
reflection on scripture. All three of the women — Katie Cannon,
Renita Weems, and Jacquelyn Grant — wrote with the authority
of their scholarly backgrounds. That they were also grounded in
their faith traditions added power to their voices. All of their works
were infused with social criticism, which is in-depth analysis of the
signs of the times. Social criticism has since become a significant
component of womanist theology. Each woman's work represented
the culmination of dialogues among black women as their work
brought to fruition ideas that had been simmering in the essays
of, among others, Toinette Eugene, Delores Williams, and Cheryl
Townsend Gilkes. Alice Walker's definition of "womanist" converged with the rise of these ideas, forming a new route for black
women to state their religious meanings. These audacious women
dared to speak from black women's perspectives. Their passion
for their work is conspicuous, indicating levels of their personal
growth as religious scholars.

"I first began pondering the relationship between faith and
ethics as a schoolgirl while listening to my grandmother teach
the central affirmation of Christianity within the context of a
racially segregated society."[1] The first words of Katie Cannon's
Black Womanist Ethics identified her own experience as motivation for her later studies. Such motivation arises for many African
Americans who are aware of the dissonances between their oppressive experiences and the mythical American dream. Dissonance is
also apparent between their life situations and the professed values of mainstream Christian faith traditions. Cannon's recollection
of her childhood queries resonates with these dissonances between
black experiences and social theories. *Black Womanist Ethics* took
important steps toward the development of a specifically stated
womanist ethics.

Cannon began the book by sketching a historical overview of
the moral situation of black women in America, especially the

burdens created by the social institutions of enslavement and Jim Crow. The interconnected race, class, and gender oppressions that black women continue to experience have deep roots in these structures. "Both in the informal day-to-day life and the formal organization and institutions in society Black women are still the victims of the aggravated inequities of the tridimensional phenomenon of race/class/gender oppression."[2] Drawing a parallel between the history and the literary tradition of African American women, Cannon analyzed Zora Neale Hurston's earlier twentieth-century literature and life to further develop ideas of a womanist ethics.

Cannon's writing signaled new beginnings in several ways. She launched her work from the perspectives of black women's truths, long overlooked as a location from which to begin an ethical study. In that process, Cannon reconsidered history, thereby demonstrating the differences that black women's concrete experiences create for such basic ethical frameworks as moral values and judgments. By valuing black women's experiences, she challenged the basic assumptions of white, male, Christian ethics about individuals, personal and communal power, and acts of choice. Using Zora Neale Hurston's literature and life, Cannon pointed to the potential of black literary traditions for social analysis. For all the wonder of Hurston's writing, her life was overlaid with tragedy: she was not accepted by black communities or male colleagues or protected by the white literary establishment. In this telling, Cannon lifted up the dangers for black women intellectuals even while recognizing the authority of black women's lives and literature. Questions of authority are important in this work, for Cannon centered the ideas of two black theologians, Martin Luther King Jr. and Howard Thurman. Such a process continues in research by black scholars who seek sources from the intellectual traditions of the black community. What validates the truths of our lives? Cannon utilized Hurston, King, and Thurman as some authorities for the construction of womanist thought. Cannon's work of womanist ethics raised the rigor of black women's religious research to new levels, setting standards that resonated with their experiences.

If Cannon's work brought new levels to rigorous, scholarly research, Renita Weems's approach added something different to the womanist conversation. Today it is necessary to recall — with multiple sources of inspirational material for and by black women, from Oprah's magazine to Iyanla Vanzant's best-selling reflections — that the mid-1980s offered very little scriptural or pastoral material from these perspectives. In *Just a Sister Away: A Womanist Vision of Women's Relationships in the Bible,* Weems's pastoral focus utilized theological reflection directed toward the needs of African American women. In the foreword, Weems wrote:

> If, like myself, you are an African-American woman, you are all the more hungry to hear a voice you recognize. How many times have I gone into bookstores — feminist, African-American, and Christian bookstores — desperately seeking a book written unapologetically with me, an African-American woman, in mind. . . . *Just a Sister Away* is an *audacious* attempt to probe beneath the surface of biblical texts to discover a place for everyone in the Kingdom.[3]

Weems, as a biblical scholar, drew on contemporary feminist literature and combined it with womanist scholarship in order to speak to black women's needs. She interpreted nine biblical stories featuring women, beginning with Hagar's: "For black women, the story of Hagar in the Old Testament book of Genesis is a haunting one."[4] Through her interpretation of the story, Weems related black women's oppression and exploitation with that of the slave Hagar. Weems deepens the analysis by presenting American capitalism's effects on black women as another form of rape and enslavement. Each biblical story Weems interpreted embraced an aspect of women's lives, such as friendship, mourning, and in-laws. In this way, concerns of contemporary women were connected with the stories of women in the Bible and became a rich source for theological reflection.

An important womanist focus that Weems sharpened is the need to remain connected to the community of black women as a component of research. This is not a simple task: *either* pastoral life *or* the academic world makes significant demands on the professional's time. For scholars of religion, the connections between faith practice and theological reflection within the enterprise of theology are of critical importance, but are also a logistical nightmare. Weems attempts to bridge the gap, directing her work to African

American women who are not necessarily in the academy, while using her academic skills.

In *White Women's Christ, Black Women's Jesus,* Jacquelyn Grant took on the dual tasks of refining the unique mode of womanist theology while simultaneously applying the ideas to the construction of a christology. The contrast that Grant sets up in the very title of the work — of Christ, a conceptual term, or Jesus, a personalized name — presents a sharp theological contrast that distinguishes white and black women's religious thinking. Grant begins the book with a presentation of the framework of feminist theology, which she contends is firmly rooted in white American women's experiences. She challenges the racism she identifies as embedded in feminist theology: "White women have defined the [feminist] movement and presumed to do so not only for themselves but also for non-White women. They have misnamed themselves by calling themselves feminists when in fact they are White feminists."[5] Grant contends that black women cannot really call themselves "black feminists" as this is a contradiction in terms. If white women's experience is the ground for feminist theology, then it follows that black women's experiences will yield a different theology, which is womanist.

Utilizing the then-emerging writing and research of African American women, Grant identifies womanist theology as experientially based. "[Womanist] accents our being responsible, in charge, outrageous and audacious enough to demand the right to think theologically and to do it independently of both White and Black men and White women."[6]

Grant throws out three challenges for womanist theologians based mostly on black women's needs and partially on the inadequacy of feminist theology. The shortcomings she finds in feminist statements of christology are centered on the embedded racism and rejection of black women's realities that are found in white women's lives. Related to these shortcomings, she identifies theological challenges for womanists. The first is to

> investigate the relationship between the oppression of women and theological symbolism. . . . The second challenge for Black women is we must explore more deeply the question of

what Christ means in a society in which class distinctions are increasing. If Christ is among "the least" then who are they?...The third and final challenge for Black women is to do constructive Christology, a liberating one, for both the Black women's community and the larger Black community. A Christology which negates Black male humanity is still destructive to the Black community.[7]

In this short passage, Grant lays out an agenda that has been important to womanists in the ensuing years: a close analysis of African American women's experiences of oppression in all its forms; a focus on new ways to theologically define and understand Christ, especially in light of class issues; and the development of a holistic christology. Grant's clear vision of challenges to be addressed by womanist scholars was prophetic, and womanist scholars are continuing to answer the deeper questions she has asked. Some of the issues raised by her work will be addressed in more detail in a later chapter.

These three works are noted because each set a tone and framework for the development of womanist theology. Inherent in these works are several of the components of womanist theology that were delineated at the end of chapter 3. These components include reclamation of historically grounded analytical approaches to the ways that black women name God and the development of new ways to listen to black women's voices. The basis for their research then opened a rich vein of possibility as these three authors drew from the many meanings of faith in African American women's lives to assess institutional, social, and doctrinal structures. They indicated the operations of the ordinary theologies of black women's daily lives as rich sources for theological constructions, emphasizing the importance of spiritual and communal life. These themes become the basis for understanding the unique approaches that womanists use in developing theology.

Other disciplines' inclusion of black women's voices was an additional factor in shaping those distinctive approaches to theology. This is an important point alluded to earlier and is grounds for discussing womanist theology as interdisciplinary. In other words, womanist thought did not develop in a vacuum. Like other forms of liberation theology, womanist theology made the deliberate connection between life and religious thought, or practice and theory; the ideas of black women intellectuals from other disciplines provided authoritative arguments from African American women's standpoints. Their work particularly deconstructed black women's social worlds within the framework of the dominant society. Two thinkers, one from sociology and one from history, provide important examples of these facts.

In 1990 Patricia Hill Collins, a sociologist, published *Black Feminist Thought: Knowledge, Consciousness, and the Politics of Empowerment.* In this important text, Collins established the realities of a black women's point of view, an epistemology. Epistemology is the framework from which each person can claim to know. What is true? What is real? How does anyone know? The unique life experiences of black women created frameworks of knowledge that are different from those of the dominant society. Collins utilized historic and contemporary research that demonstrated clearly the distinctive meaning-worlds born from African American women's experiences. These experiences, in turn, become the intellectual parameters from which black women interpret reality and make decisions. Further, Collins presents descriptions of these realities. Collins, however, firmly remains a black feminist and challenges the construction of "womanist."[8] Collins is not the only black sociologist considering the dynamics of black women's lives. Sociology questions the structures of social knowledge, peering beneath vernacular understandings of human institutions. These types of study, which give honest and sometimes painful definition to black women, are critically important to shaping womanist theology.

Darlene Clark Hine edited the several volumes of *Black Women in American History*[9] in 1990, writing black women back into history. Hine is noted for her own abilities as a scholar who utilizes primary documents to interpret black women's history.[10] Her work is in dialogue with other black women historians who authenticate the historic roots of contemporary American history, including the ongoing invisibility of black women. Their work places the overlooked lives of African American women in prominent positions within the tapestry of American history.[11]

The few books on black women in the mainstream press had begun to multiply by the mid-1980s, rapidly expanding by the mid-1990s. The earlier writings by Cannon, Weems, and Grant had been somewhat limited by the lack of availability of resources about black women. Conversely, this fact heightens the importance of their achievements: they were pioneers who became the resources. By the early 1990s, research such as Collins's and Hine's meant that womanist theologians and ethicists had new material from which to draw.

The works of black women, whether womanist or black feminist, were closely allied in their aims. Theories were intended to empower and influence other people, certainly beyond the academy. In a later work, *Fighting Words: Black Women and the Search for Justice,* Patricia Hill Collins uses three questions to review any social theory, questions that can also be applied to the womanist theological theories: "Does this social theory speak the truth to people about the reality of their lives? . . . Does this social theory equip people to resist oppression? . . . Does this theory move people to struggle?"[12] These motivations of truth, resistance, and struggle will be seen in the distinctive approaches to theology that womanists continued to develop during the 1990s.

Distinctive Approaches

By the early 1990s, the availability of resources and networking among womanist religious thinkers created the options for distinctive approaches to developing theology and ethics. Several works are noted in order to point out the distinctive approaches to theology that womanist starting points and hermeneutics helped to shape. Emilie Townes, Marcia Riggs, and Katie Cannon contributed to the nurturance of womanist theologians through publication of several works. That all three women are ethicists emphasizes several points made in the previous chapter.

In 1993, Emilie Townes's *Womanist Justice, Womanist Hope*[13] took womanist ethics further on a path that was grounded in history. Like Cannon's use of Zora Neale Hurston's life story, Townes drew from the often-overlooked history of Ida Wells Barnett. Wells

Barnett was significant in bringing worldwide attention to the ter-
rorist lynchings of black people during the nineteenth century.
Two thousand lynchings were recorded between 1880 and 1900.
The bold actions of an African American woman of the past became Townes's basis of considering black women's work for social
justice. Her work also showed the basis on which black women
construct the concept of justice.

The following year, Townes edited a volume entitled *A Troubling in My Soul: Womanist Perspectives on Evil and Suffering*.[14]
The contributors demonstrated the collaboration among womanist thinkers, some of whom are ethicists, theologians, and pastors.
Some utilized personal reflection or drew from the disciplines of
history or sociology to construct their ideas. The various contributors continued Jacquelyn Grant's challenge to analyze the suffering
in black women's lives. This book became a forum on suffering and
evil, related to a larger study of salvation. How do black women
experience suffering? What are the kinds of suffering that black
women experience, and how does this link with spirituality? *How*
does God save from the oppressions known to black women?

In 1994, Marcia Riggs's *Awake, Arise, and Act: A Womanist
Call for Black Liberation*[15] began the difficult work of analyzing the meanings of social stratification within African American
communities today. Like Cannon, Weems, and Grant, she has em-
barked on a journey that does not always have clear signposts. A
thorough analysis of class internal to black communities is defi-
nitely needed, especially if placed in relationship with the wider
socioeconomic world. This is an area of womanist theology and
ethics that continues to demand attention, and Riggs has led the
way in formulating the issues. She has prophetically charged the
black community to define a "socioreligious moral vision for the
twenty-first century." Drawing from the black women's club movement of the nineteenth century, Riggs identifies three moral virtues
from the clubwomen's work for justice: renunciation (selflessness),
inclusivity (community-building), and responsibility (focusing on
mission). These elements are important to the development of
communal values for contemporary times.[16]

Emilie Townes published *In a Blaze of Glory: Womanist Spirituality as Social Witness* in 1995.[17] Her work explored a deeper

understanding of African American women's embodied realities, one that does not divorce body and spirit. This has particular implications for defining black women's moral values, providing one authoritative basis for comprehending womanist spirituality. Townes defines this spirituality as "the deep kneading of humanity and divinity into one breath, one hope, one vision. Womanist spirituality is not only a way of living, it is a style of witness that seeks to cross the yawning chasm of hatreds and prejudices and oppressions into a deeper and richer love of God."[18] She conceptually links the social activism of black women with spirituality in a holistic and integrative view.

In addition, in 1995, *Katie's Canon: Womanism and the Soul of the Black Community*[19] was published. Katie Cannon continued exploration of her earlier work, *Black Womanist Ethics,* granting much greater definition to both ethics and womanist religious thought. Cannon expanded her statement of the meanings of virtue in black women's lives. She revisited slave narratives, continuing the use of historical recovery of black women's intellectual riches. She raised other aspects of race and economics using the ideas of an early-twentieth-century black economist. Probably the most critical contribution of this collection is Cannon's outline of womanist methodology for doing ethics, which will be discussed in the next section of this chapter.

The contributions of these womanist thinkers stand as proof of an earlier claim that womanist ethics is the starting point of womanist theology. This ethics-first approach, based on the texts of African American women's lives, considers power relationships in society, deconstructs oppressions, and provides new paradigms for thinking about "the way things always are." From these analyses, new resources can be identified, especially in the processes of giving voice to ordinary theologies of black women's daily lives through both historical and contemporary investigation. Uncovering or stating implicit values that reside in historical and contemporary African American women's lives becomes a strong basis for the methodological development that will be discussed in the next section.

Most important, through the authority of ethics, black women have been able to develop autonomous voices. Although ignorance and stereotype are backdrops against which black women constantly play, the movement to self-defined voices indicates that black women can choose when and whether to respond to socially negative images. For clarity, it must be stated that womanist ethics developed concurrently with womanist theology: networking among these thinkers continues to produce womanist books and articles. Written for black women, most often by other black women, these works adopt a proactive theoethical stance: instead of constant refutation of negative studies, the energy of these scholars flows into the creation of personally meaningful explorations of their religious meanings. Determining how and where one stands, instead of accepting an assigned place, is self-empowerment. From this position, womanists enter constructive theological dialogues.

Developing Methods of Womanist Work

Method is the deliberative process of argumentation or exploration of different aspects of faith that lead toward theological theories. Methodologies for womanists reflect multiple academic disciplines. Womanist theology, by centering the lives and experiences of black women, has a methodological starting point of the human person — hence, the emphasis on multiple disciplines and related ethical analysis. Womanist theology begins with these life experiences and ordinary theologies to name the location of holiness in black women's lives.

Methodologies are not benign: scholars have commitments in their work. Generally, the commitments of womanist scholars include, among others: centering black women's experience; social analysis of the black community's condition; exploring the authentic shape of African American religious life; deconstruction of all oppressions that stunt human growth. Reaching this level of commitment does not happen accidentally; arriving at this place becomes part of the methodology itself. Therefore, as part of the method, womanists will often spend time stating portions of their own autobiographies. This disclosure names their formation processes and their resultant commitments as theologians or ethicists.

The hunger and need to express black women's realities in the light of faith are powerful motivations to step into the streams of womanist thought. The continued marginalization of black women with personal experiences of oppression is a powerful incentive to think again about God's action in daily life. Questions drive the analysis that many African American women have already learned to utilize in daily life. Why are things the way they are? Who has power and who does not? Who created the situation? What is being done now or should be done to change these present situations? The methodology of womanist theology systematizes these questions, seeking not mere theory at the ending, but plans of action.

Naming methodologies creates greater authority for the work of womanists: rather than the ravings of half-mad women, womanist ethics and theology can be considered scholarly partners in rigorous scholarship. However, the multilevel construction processes of womanist religious thought require a creative approach to method, recovering lost visions and making sense of them.

The processes of piecing facts and visions together, of methodically doing womanist theology, can be likened to playing jazz music. Jazz is not a simple form of music, as some believe, not understanding that the artistry can create an illusion of ease. Neither is jazz undisciplined or lacking in form — as some believe womanist theology lacks rigor and structure. Jazz relies on the talents of each member in a group, with varied instruments that must be played together in sets that match. Individual skill does not stand alone, but works within cooperative arrangements. Womanist theologians work cooperatively, in seemingly informal ways.

Jazz is often difficult to learn, especially the art of improvisation, which has a variety of patterns that must be learned before the musician can begin to appear "free" or fit in with the other artists in playing the music. It is especially difficult for the person who cannot get "off the page" of written music. Certainly, jazz is related to other forms of music, but there is a uniqueness to its own structure. In like manner, womanists have moved from the written pages of church doctrine or North Atlantic theological traditions to name something that is unique to the experiences and meanings of black women.

One element of becoming skilled in jazz is "audiation," a technical musical term that describes musical listening with the inner, creative ear to notes that are not on the written page; it is related to the ability to create and remember melodies internally. It is almost an intuitive art. Some jazz artists have never learned to read music but are able to hear and play it. Like jazz, as womanist theologians continue to notate the audiation and perfect the techniques, the form will become more established, and the techniques — or methods — will become more formal.

Several authors have begun to refine the technique and method of doing womanist ethics and theology, following the methodology detailed by Katie Cannon. There are six stages to the process Cannon envisions. The womanist ethicist/theologian should utilize an emancipatory historiography, uncover theological resources and disciplines, clarify the operative norms, identify strategic options, announce and celebrate the conclusions reached, and then begin to analyze again. Cannon pictures this as a circular process.[20] For this text, the process can be considered an opportunity for improvisational artistry, demanding technical skill. A closer look at the process that Cannon outlines will make this connection with jazz clearer.

Emancipatory historiography analyzes the historical roots of oppression. Such a reading of history — through the eyes of black women — provides a realistic context of the roots of oppression. When current realities are linked to root historical events (sometimes called a "reflexive" process), it is possible for the theorist to avoid essentializing black women's experiences. Sounding the second note of theological resources and disciplines will either support or challenge the understandings of the oppressions. This grounds the historical data in real social structures, for resources include social institutions or movements (family, church, business, education, nation, and so on), in addition to religious traditions. In this way, definitions of reality from the perspective of the oppressed begin to take shape.

Next, the clarification of norms identifies the underlying values that support the alternative knowledge that the community holds. Then, strategic options reflect on the history, values, and theoethical insights from the above process and hark back to the wider community to begin an exploration of the possibilities for justice and systemic change. Annunciation and celebration, the fifth component in Cannon's schema, bring the theories and proposals into dialogue with members of the community, who are asked to validate or negate the findings of the study. Finally, re-reflection and strategic action, now possible because of this interchange between theory and practice, can affirm previous findings or become opportunities to recognize dissonances, and then the process begins again.

An example of such methodology can be seen in ethicist Joan M. Martin's *More Than Chains or Toil: A Christian Work Ethic of Enslaved Women.*[21] Martin utilizes enslaved women's narratives as an interpretive lens. She states:

> Enslaved women's narratives *set free* the lives of women who were propertied objects and artifacts of others' history; the narratives made them the subjects of history. They provide a source of enslaved witnessing which can be characterized both as an individual document and as a wide-ranging, broad corpus of autobiographical and narrative writing that includes journals, newspaper articles, magazine interviews, church records, personal letters, and amanuensic autobiographies of ex-enslaved women and men. Narratives reveal the institution of slavery as experienced by enslaved people.[22]

Martin taps into historical narratives of enslaved women, centering and making visible black women's experiences. As she develops her framework, this becomes a form of emancipatory historiography locating roots of oppression. She does not raise the lives of black women as exhibits for curiosity's sake but to clarify operative norms. Scripture, doctrine, and tradition are brought into dialogue with black women's experiences. Naming this process womanist "theoethics," Martin further defines the objectives: "Womanist theological and ethical praxis endeavors to speak of a multidimensional tradition within African American Christianity.... For womanist theo-ethicist thinkers, historicity and hermeneutics must begin with black women's existence in and experience of slavery."[23] Martin identifies the legacy of an enslaved women's work ethic and then links it to contemporary African

American women with her theoethical insights and suggestions for action.

Other womanists present different visions of methodology. As we have seen, Renita Weems employed a narrative methodology. Her approach to constructing womanist theology resonates with African American traditions of oral culture. Other womanist thinkers utilized literary tools in their methodology, as did Katie Cannon when she focused on Zora Neale Hurston's work. Townes's *Troubling in My Soul* is truly like a jazz improvisation, where each artist takes a solo on the theme. The methodologies used by womanists aim to continue the processes of defining, naming, shaping, responding to, and otherwise creating the rich dimensions of African American women's religious lives.

At its heart, womanist methodology remains resistance-oriented. It serves as a way to resist being excluded from research, to resist dehumanizing definitions of black people, and to resist invisibility. The power to resist comes from vision. Emilie Townes names the framework of resistance when she discusses "the apocalyptic womanist vision":

> The apocalyptic vision evolves from crisis and martyrdom. It is a theo-ethical, sociopolitical manifesto that refuses to accept or tolerate injustice.... Apocalyptic vision in a womanist mode is rooted in the movement of history for African American women and me.... The apocalyptic vision that demands a cold, hard womanist stare at suffering rejects its inevitability and chooses life over extinction.[24]

Continued Development of Womanist Theology

So far, this chapter's explorations of womanist constructions have taken a route through signal texts, ethical analyses, and distinctions of womanist methodologies. These steps turn toward the most significant womanist theology text to date, Delores Williams's *Sisters in the Wilderness: The Challenge of Womanist God-Talk*, which was published in 1993. Cited in the previous chapter,

William's identification of the defining characteristics of womanist theology bears repeating:

> Womanist theology attempts to help black women see, affirm and have confidence in the importance of their experience and faith for determining the character of the Christian religion in the African-American community. Womanist theology challenges all oppressive forces impeding black women's struggle for survival and for the development of a positive, productive quality of life conducive to women's and the family's freedom and well-being. Womanist theology opposes all oppression based on race, sex, class, sexual preference, physical disability and caste.... Womanist theology ... also branches off in its own direction, introducing new issues and constructing new analytical categories.[25]

Several notes resound in this excerpt. Womanist theology is for black women, is grounded in experience and faith, and analyzes the interconnecting oppressions of race, class, gender, and all other forms. Womanist theology may set off in new directions, with new words and ideas that are resonant with the lives of black women. Within this brief description, the African American community is central and the very basis for womanist thought.

Williams states some of the basic premises for womanist theology throughout *Sisters in the Wilderness*. She begins her construction with a grounding in the black religious tradition by using the figure of Hagar. Hagar's importance for black women's religiosity is emphasized in this work, as it was in Renita Weems's *Just a Sister Away*. Hagar was an Egyptian slave in Abram's household, forced by the manipulations of his wife, Sarai, to bear Abram's son. When Hagar attempted to escape, an angel of God returned her to her captors' camp. Abraham's wife eventually gave birth, so the slave Hagar and her son were rejected, unwanted, and cast into the desert. In the midst of her turmoil, Hagar conversed with God in the wilderness (Gen. 16:1–16; 21:1–21). Williams connects this story to that of black women who also experience wilderness times. The themes of the meaning of motherhood, poverty and homelessness, the expendability of black women and children, and the ongoing use of black women's bodies for assorted forms of surrogacy correlate the story of Hagar with African American women's experiences.

The Hagar story and its place in black women's lives, Williams points out, have a long history in black communities and set the framework for an African American women's religious tradition. Williams states: "Even today, most of Hagar's situation is congruent with [that of] many African-American women.... Many black women have testified that 'God helped them make a way out of no way.' The female-centered tradition of African-American biblical appropriation could be named the *survival/quality-of-life tradition.*"[26]

Williams explicitly connects survival and quality of life, a revolutionary concept in the ordinary theologies of black women. No simple or clear-cut redemptive moment occurred for Hagar; rather, the miracle *is* survival, and it continues in contemporary black women's experiences. What does it mean to survive in the middle of oppressions? How does God save? What does liberation mean to black women? The burdens of the survival of both family and community have often fallen on women. In fact, African American women's survival skills can become gateways for liberation. However, the revolutionary point is that such survival skills cannot be viewed in isolation. Survival is connected to a living faith and awareness of some Greater Power in operation in one's life. To repeat Delores Williams's words, "Many black women have testified that 'God helped them make a way out of no way.'... The female-centered tradition of African-American biblical appropriation could be named the *survival/quality-of-life* tradition." The quality-of-life dimensions are witnessed in black women's activism on behalf of family or community and are integral to the creation of communities. The quality-of-life tradition is reflected in many black women's stories, such as the women of the Detroit Metropolitan Black Women's Health Project. Here, in the connections of survival and quality of life, is what Townes terms the "apocalyptic vision."

Delores Williams's *Sisters in the Wilderness* remains a demanding book in its thoroughness and scope. Williams drew from multiple sources including history, church tradition, scripture, and political analysis to highlight facets of womanist theology. In the

process, she faced head-on difficult issues that cause unease with
traditional faith in its comfortable garb. What about those black
churches that oppress the women members? How should we begin
to think about black women's reproductive rights? Who is Jesus for
black women? All these questions form her deliberative theological analysis: Williams does just what she charges other womanist
theologians to do, that is, to "begin raising questions about the analytical appropriateness of all traditional doctrinal categories for
interrogating African-American women's experience — questions
that trouble the theological waters."[27]

Williams clearly states that her work is not a complete systematic theology, as she may only surface questions but not necessarily
arrive at answers. Ambiguity is part of the process of womanist theology, in fact may be critical to its growth. Simultaneously,
many of the constructions Williams uses serve as foundations for
building other layers of womanist theology. Williams puts both
these ideas into a frame when she writes:

> As black women retrieving our experience from "invisibil-
> ity," each of us retrieves from the underside of the underside
> partial facts about ourselves and partial visions of missing
> parts of our experience. So in theology, our womanist work
> together is to connect these pieces of fact and vision.[28]

Williams presents these different womanist visions as parts of a
mosaic that will express many facets of black women's experiences.
She delineates her own commitments in her work:

> I think we womanist theologians ... do not lose our intention
> for black women's experience to provide the lens through
> which we view sources, to provide the issues that form the
> content of our theology and to help us formulate the ques-
> tions we ask about God's relation to black American life and
> to the world in general.... Our purpose is to present more
> precisely what African-American women and the African-
> American community have and do believe and to exercise
> a prophetic womanist theological task in relation to this
> belief.[29]

The idea of a prophetic theological task repositions theology as a project that responds to needs, is grounded in belief in God and love of the community, and, therefore, is responsible to each. Theology, in this womanist view, is an inclusive process.

Williams's concepts offer an epistemological framework through which to consider the discussions of womanist theology in the following chapters. She, with the other womanist thinkers in this chapter, developed methods aiming to view black women, God, churches, and communities as linked. Drawing upon social analysis may deconstruct some sacred groves, but provides exciting opportunities for new growth. This is a powerful process, a prophetic task. In the words of another womanist theologian, Diana L. Hayes:

> Womanist theologians seek a better world for all of God's people, regardless of race, gender, ethnicity, class, or sexual orientation. Their immediate goal is to reclaim the voices of black women in order to help strengthen and rebuild the black community. Their ultimate goal is the development of a theology that liberates all people.[30]

Discussion Questions

1. Explain the relationships between methodology and commitments, using the authors in this chapter as examples.

2. Can you think of a story of an African American woman who overcame great odds? (This need not be a well-known person.) What do you think are the values that informed her life? Why?

3. Contrast the story above with a situation comedy on television that features black women.

4. Select one of the quotes used in this chapter and define the methodology used.

Chapter 5

Dialogue and
Womanist Theology

Chapter 3 set up the defining parameters of womanist theology, and chapter 4 stressed the importance of methodology in womanist constructions. This chapter considers one constitutive component of womanist method: dialogical processes. Delores Williams aptly termed these processes the "dialogical intent" of womanist theology.[1]

The womanist commitment to dialogue is not merely professional good manners. Rather, four aims are reflected. First, networking is a component of black women's epistemological frameworks. Networking defines both the community and the individual: "I" becomes more distinct in community. Dialogue is a form of networking. Second, the womanist commitment to ending oppression for all requires community building, which in turn requires dialogue with all the members. Next, alliances are necessary for all those who are committed to working for justice. Finally, shaping womanist theology is a process within permeable boundaries, not just in ivory towers. This process of dialogue is not easily accomplished and can become a balancing act. Several perspectives will clarify these points.

Sheron C. Patterson's *New Faith: A Black Christian Woman's Guide to Reformation, Re-creation, Rediscovery, Renaissance, Resurrection, and Revival* discusses womanist theology in contrast to black or feminist theologies. "Imagine this: A question is presented to you, but before you can answer it, an Anglo woman or man or an African American man speaks on your behalf. Your opinions are not heard and do not matter.... Let us be in charge of our theology."[2] The distinctiveness of black women's experiences requires speaking on our own behalf. Yet the temptation to slide into a kind of relativism draws all religious scholars; tolerating another's point of view can be a way to avoid difficult discussions. Delores Williams presents a way to consider the challenges of dialogue: "Womanist theologians can invite feminist, black liberation and other interested theologians to engage with them in the exploration of the question: What is God's word about survival and quality of life formation for oppressed and quasi-free people struggling to build community in the wilderness?"[3] The processes of exploring questions have their own temptations, including rushing to judgment of others' ideas or compromising beliefs for the sake of a mythical unity. What is at stake in the balancing act of dialogue is the integrity of womanist intellectual life.

This chapter considers several dialogues that occur as womanist theologians continue to speak on our own behalf. The conversations are not always easy and are often inconclusive. These conversations point out in particular the wealth of different intellectual strands within black communities. There is no single belief system for all black people, and there are many efforts underway to end oppressions. Womanist dialogues are occurring with black feminists and white feminists, with Afrocentrists and black male theologians, with church members and students, and with women across the African Diaspora. All of these conversations aid in constructions of womanist theology.

Womanist or Black Feminist? Naming Ourselves

The question comes in almost any initial discussion of womanism: Why don't you just call yourself black feminist? The ongoing conversations between black feminists and womanists are important because they are intellectual routes by which black women discuss their own identities. It is not a totally new dialogue, but is heightened now as black women get a toehold in the academy and publishing. Both terms — womanist and black feminist — locate ways to identify important dimensions of black women's lives. Depending on the discipline, the term chosen can open to strategic alliances or become an analytical tool.

Many dynamics are at play in conversations between black feminists and womanists. The dialogue between womanists and black feminists is ongoing, with multiple sites of conflict and congruence. The conflict comes from within the community of African American women intellectuals as they debate the possibilities for the genuine development of scholarship that can influence black communities.

Black feminism has had a longer development in different disciplines than has womanism. Images of black women began appearing in *Ms.* magazine during the 1970s. Black women were beginning to redefine ourselves in relationship to the black community, daring to speak for themselves. In the late twentieth century, feminism did give black women a public platform from which to speak. But the concept of feminism itself was burdened by the nineteenth-century split between black and white women; the black women's club movement became the separated platform for public service. Certainly black women have a long history of being public speakers with the aims of changing unjust social structures:

> That God called black women like Sojourner Truth (c. 1799–1883) and Maria Stewart to preach and teach against injustice did not shield them from mockery, suspicion, and censure. Stewart, the first American-born woman to speak in public in Boston (1832), claimed that God gave her the "spirit of independence" to proclaim a message of spiritual regeneration through community reform.[4]

Black and white American women developed different styles of activism. Generally, black women have an activist agenda that adopts a feminist or womanist stance. In spite of this, the dialogues between black feminists and womanists retain some flavor of the past. Is it legitimate for black women to claim feminism for themselves? After all, the memory lingers: white women activists rejected working with black women, and white women who were beneficiaries of patriarchy were not to be trusted. Many African American women retain distrust of white women's motives today. (These issues will resurface in the dialogues between white feminists and womanists.) To many African American women, adopting the name "black feminist" seems to allow white feminists to retain control, but black feminists would certainly disagree with this assessment. Yet the questions linger in black communities: If a black woman calls herself a "feminist," does she hate black men? Would she destroy the black community?

And for some black feminists, the new name "womanist" seems an evasion of the harder discussions that need to take place. Use of the term also seems to indicate a genuine loss because it seems to cede "ownership" of feminism to white women. Additionally, black feminists ask what type of intellectual rigor a womanist uses. Isn't womanism just an extension of black, male-controlled thinking? (There is spillover of these ideas in the dialogues between womanists and Afrocentrists.) These questions, linked with a history of distrust, often create awkward situations in dialogue between womanists and black feminists. There are features of the dialogue, however, that should be considered.

Most womanist/black feminist discussions occur within the academy. As a consequence, the black women who are making a choice between the designations "womanist" and "black feminist" are also working within specific academic disciplines. Black women in some disciplines are more likely to designate themselves black feminists, and others, notably those working in theology and ethics, identify themselves as womanists. Either of these indicates something important about the scholar who is seeking safe spaces and support, formally or informally, for her intellectual work. Mutuality among black women scholars becomes a mode of sustaining and refining research in a given field. These formal or informal connections are continuations of black women's networking traditions. Yet variations among black feminists' and womanists' views sometimes increase tensions and confusion.

The difficulties in the ongoing womanist/black feminist dialogues are exemplified by a commentary on womanist thought by Patricia Hill Collins in which she is both critical and complimentary of the womanist concept. Collins herself is firmly committed as a sociologist to the concept of black feminism and, from this perspective, critiques the weaknesses of the idea of womanism. She states that there are flaws in Alice Walker's definition of woman-

ist because it constructs a universalized definition of black women,
thereby creating an essentializing category. The Walker definition
further "presents womanism as different from and superior to
feminism, a difference allegedly stemming from Black and White
women's different histories within American racism."[5] Collins's
critique charges that Walker's definition utilizes outdated black
nationalist arguments of separatism and empowerment, that its different sections are contradictory, and that it works against women.
On the other hand, Collins identifies the positive perspectives in the
womanist concept as she considers the work of womanist ethicists:

> Black women theorists have been attracted to the joining of
> pluralism and racial integration of this [pluralistic] interpre-
> tation of Walker's womanism. Black women theologians, in
> particular, illustrate this use. As an ethical system, woman-
> ism is always in the making — it is not a closed fixed system
> of ideas but one that continually evolves through its rejec-
> tion of all forms of oppression and its commitment to social
> justice.[6]

Collins's comments on womanist thought indicate the complex discussions among black women scholars who seek to shape their
disciplines and to name themselves in the process. Her comments
bring into relief the reality that the lines of demarcation between
black feminist and womanist are often blurred.

Joy James is a cultural theorist who has mapped a useful range
of black feminisms, of which womanist thought is one form. She
offers a much more productive method of discussing the differences
between womanists and black feminists by considering all such
theorists along a continuum of thought. Along this continuum,
Collins, Walker, and bell hooks give rise to different expressions
of black feminism:

> To some degree then, we can distinguish between a con-
> ventional feminism embraceable by all progressive women,
> including those who happen to be black, and a black fem-
> inism or womanism, one particular to women of African
> descent. Yet there is a third form of feminism applicable only

to those black women who are left of liberal or stand outside conventional politics.[7]

James's different vision draws from the political implications of different black feminisms, and she sounds a caution against simplistic definitions. Her vision refers to potential mutuality among the various forms of black feminism along the continuum. She also warns about the ways that black feminist ideas are sometimes commodified in a market economy, resulting in essentialized black women. Market success of the very idea of black feminism may work to its detriment, James claims. "Marketed as exotica, black feminist sensibilities and literature often appear as a source of emotive stories of feminine colored pain and ethnic eccentricities for consumers."[8]

The dialogue between womanists and black feminists will certainly continue. Both womanist theologians and black feminists benefit from these dialogues. Black feminists became one of the initial dialogical partners as womanist theologians began to identify themselves. The processes of self-naming continue, as both black feminists and womanists refine their understandings of black women within their various disciplines. The research of black feminists and womanists is exchanged in the shared commitments to analyze and deconstruct, at the least, race, gender, and class constructions. As a result, the new constructions of these scholars within different disciplines are strengthened.

Dialogue between Womanists and White Feminists

Katie Cannon has written, "Black women are repeatedly asked to cast our lot of identifying loyalties in one or another competing camp. Either we are Blacks or we are women."[9] The tensions that many womanists experience revolve around such questions of loyalty. Dialogue between womanists and white feminists assists in drawing conceptual distinctions between the two. Both are hampered in their ability to fully listen to the other.

Elisabeth Schüssler Fiorenza, a leading feminist biblical scholar, wrote in 1993 of these tensions:

> More and more the diverse resistant discourses of emerg-
> ing feminist political movements around the world interrupt
> those discourses of gender studies that conceptualize feminist
> interpretation as the practice of reading *as a woman.* These
> political discourses challenge Western universalist claims that
> all women have a special, essential nature in common and
> that all women are defined in the same way in their otherness
> to men. If feminist theology should displace the kyriarchal
> "politics of submission and otherness," it can no longer
> construct women's identity as unitary.[10]

However, womanist scholars enter this dialogue with some unease, knowing that not all white feminist scholars are as open as
Fiorenza's words invite them to be. If we are in charge of our theology, as Sheron Patterson encourages womanists, then how much
exchange should take place with white feminists? Should womanists limit dialogue with white feminists? Katie Cannon's personal
experience leads her to ask these questions:

> By using the scholarship of White feminist liberationists to
> frame and substantiate the theoretical requisites for rejecting
> patriarchal intrusions in the predicament of African American
> women, am I running the risk of lobotomizing womanist ethics
> and diminishing both Black women agents and agency? . . . Is
> it appropriate for Black women to use analytical modes of
> exposing and criticizing domination and exploitation created
> by women with different social identities?[11]

Cannon's sentiments fairly shout through this selection, but the
questions of legitimacy and validation become part of the dialogue
with feminists. The tendency to locate black women's experiences
within an all-encompassing "woman" category is a universalizing
tendency that is embedded in educational and religious institutions.

The womanist project inspires passion and commitment. How
close is too close? When do womanists begin to lose our identity? There are no easy answers to these questions. Instead, women

scholars committed to liberation are meeting the challenges of working collaboratively, with few guidelines, on a daily basis.

One example of such collaboration between feminist and womanist scholars appears in the book *Feminist and Womanist Pastoral Theology*, in which the editors collected the work of a variety of pastoral theologians. Among the stated goals of the book is the following: "[This book] attempts to say...here is what is different when one takes feminist and womanist theory, in all its many forms today, and mixes it with the already-hybrid discipline of pastoral theology. We see anew the world of care, faith, and reflection. We grasp life differently."[12] This text is an example of shared research interests. There is great promise of future collaboration, and continued tension, as feminist and womanist theologians continue their liberative explorations.

Afrocentricity and Womanist Theology

Committed to ending oppression among all people, womanist theologians are socially located within the fates and fortunes of black people. Since the middle of the twentieth century, black women's role in their own communities has too often been reduced to that of uncomplaining sexual partners and baby-makers. Whether in the Civil Rights or the Black Power Movements, there were many moments in which black women felt excluded from decision making or authority. As African American women develop as scholars, the drive to distinction *within* the black communities' intellectual life creates dialogue partners. There is no single strand of black scholarship. Rather, the rich textures of African American scholarship must be scrutinized from multiple points of view.[13]

The development of black studies programs in colleges in the 1960s and 1970s brought the development of one intellectual strand known as Afrocentricity, which is "a methodology, orientation or quality of thought and practice rooted in the cultural image and human interest of African people."[14] Much of the contemporary development of the concept of Afrocentricity has been undertaken by Molefi Asante, whose scholarly work grew from the Black Power Movement. He attempted to break with a white-dominated expression of life and to develop a scholarship that was centered on black people. In other words, Afrocentric thought stood in contrast to that known as Eurocentric.

Eurocentric thought is a Western, European-derived line of thinking, particularly that which identifies England, France, Germany, Italy, Spain, and Portugal as the intellectual centers that gave birth to the greatest cultures. The United States, a nation built by immigrants from Europe, came into leadership within this grouping of countries during the twentieth century. The term "Eurocentric" has become somewhat of a misnomer; the terms "Western" and "North Atlantic" better describe the groups who have placed their ideas as the greatest advances in human thinking throughout history. In most Western civilization classes, for example, historical accounts begin with the proposition that logic and philosophy were invented by the Greeks and that political sophistication came from the Romans. Such views often exclude or diminish the contributions of the rest (read, the majority) of the world. Afrocentricity deliberately works against such narrowness by placing thinking from Africa or the African Diaspora at the center, which results in a much different view. Womanist theology certainly benefits from this revisioning of meaning. However, as Lorine Cummings asserts, there are some basic areas of agreement and large areas of difference between womanism and Afrocentrism. "Womanism and Afrocentrism are compatible in that both use the African American experience as their point of departure and call for utilization of African American role models and symbols. Conceptually, however, womanism and Afrocentrism differ."[15] The extract below gives one example of the problems that have been encountered with Afrocentricity as it has developed.

A 1990 study, following the intellectual lineage of Molefi Asante, rated heterosexual relationships among black women and men.[16] The goal of the study was to determine the level of the participants' "Afrocentric cultural consciousness" in heterosexual relationships. The participants were to identify their ideal mates and answer other questions about their behavior in possible relationships. The study concluded, among other items, that the

> subjects with high Afrocentric cultural consciousness tended
> to prioritize their ideal mate in terms of emotional and intellec-

tual stimulation, commitment to the Black community, mutual respect and sharing, Black consciousness (awareness), unconditional love, and family orientation. In contrast, subjects who manifested low Afrocentric cultural consciousness prioritized such ideal mate qualities as physical attraction, competition and control, independence, sexual compatibility, financial status, emotional status, sexual conquests, and professional status [identified as "Eurocentric" qualities by the researchers].[17]

The study also reached the conclusion that the participants who were less likely to support a mate during extreme hardship had a more Eurocentric cultural orientation. Individuality, competitiveness, sexual promiscuity, and status seeking were deemed Eurocentric values. Qualities such as "unconditional love" were deemed Afrocentric. These conclusions alone adopt a vindicationist stance, which is one that seeks to prove at all costs that black people, the oppressed, are just plain better than the people who oppressed them. While this helps the oppressed feel vindicated, there are many intellectual pitfalls that result from this thinking.[18] Yet these vindicationist concepts have political and cultural currency in the wider black community. Such ideas permeate some forms of the more commercial rap music and community meetings. Woven throughout is the theme that black women have an extremely limited place in the African American community — if they are to be "good" women who support their men.

Womanist theologians have responded to these misogynist themes by critically analyzing the concepts. Delores Williams's critique of Asante's Afrocentrism is thorough and leaves no room for doubt. "First, it is thoroughly sexist."[19] Black women are practically invisible in Asante's vision, she asserts. He presented romanticized gender-role prescriptions that ring with memories of the 1960s, of righteous black men as "freedom fighters/kings" and black women as "queens." Williams states: "The gravest limitation of Asante's Afrocentrism is that its sexism and its support of male dominance make it a convenient instrument (along with white feminism) for helping to hold white male supremacy in place in the United States."[20] White feminism, she charges, can support white male supremacy by ignoring race; Afrocentrism can do so by ignoring gender. In her critique is found the womanist theological principle of concern for ending oppression of all people.

Kanishka Chowdhury is a social theorist who also critiques Asante's Afrocentrism: "The greatest danger Asante's theories pose resides not so much in their theoretical impossibilities as in their replication of the very same Western hegemonic systems that he so despises."[21] Noting the importance of Afrocentric schools in a racist society, Chowdhury calls for an intellectual shift toward what she terms "critical Afrocentrism." This will entail not just historical reconstructions focused on black people, but also comprehensive approaches to understanding the current global political economy, along with shifts in understanding the concept of race.

Williams wrote her critique in 1995, Chowdhury in 1998, and there have been other women who have directed a very critical gaze toward Afrocentricity. There have been shifts as a result of these dialogues. In Maulana Karenga's 2002 edition of *Introduction to Black Studies*, sexism is associated with racism as rooted in capitalism:

> Capitalism, then, turns relationships and parts of relationships into commodities and utilitarian arrangements. Racism engenders self-hate, self-doubt and pathological fixation on the white paradigm. And sexism encourages artificial personal power over women as a substitute for real social power over one's destiny and daily life.[22]

The same volume critiques black women's scholarship, including the failure of the theorist to be self-critical; the exclusion of race and an exclusive focus on gender; and the failure to incorporate an Afrocentric solution to gender relationships.[23] Distinctions between some types of womanist thought are included in the volume.[24] These inclusions point to ongoing dialogue between womanists and Afrocentrists, which is by no means finished.

Black Theology and Womanist Theology

Of the different types of liberative theologies, womanist theology is most closely linked with black theology. In the construction of womanist theology, with its starting point of the realities of black *women*, African American women bring new life and shape to black theology. There are some challenges inherent to this new life, as indicated by this statement by Delores Williams:

> A complete revisionist approach in these areas [incarnation, revelation, and christology, among others] of black liberation theology is needed if black women are ever to be included. Womanist theology informed by woman-inclusive wilderness experience must, in the final analysis, lead black male liberation theologians to see in their theological thinking the "male bond" between them and white males whom they identify as oppressors.[25]

Since Williams wrote these words in 1993, dialogue between womanist and black male theologians has expanded, with a commitment to construct theologies that have greater relevance to the whole of black communities, male and female. Discussions by two black male theologians emphasize the contours of the developing dialogues.

James H. Cone participated in dialogues with a variety of pastoral leaders during the 1960s. These men issued public statements about faith life and the shape of theology in African American communities. Notable among this group was the National Committee of Negro Churchmen, who, in July 1966, published a statement on black theology and black power. Black women were not part of these discussions because the operative presumption was that black men surely spoke for black women. But black women were not silent.

Those days of women's seeming absence have slowly ended as dialogue between womanist and black male theologians has expanded and become more productive. James Cone wrote at the end of the twentieth century of the womanist scholars' contributions:

> Womanist theologians broke the monopoly of black male theological discourse. They challenged the male advocates of black theology to broaden their narrow focus on race and liberation and to incorporate gender, class, and sexuality critiques and the themes of survival and quality of life in our theological discourse.[26]

Cone links the work of womanist scholars with that of "second-generation black male theologians, biblical scholars, and historians" who do not merely parrot the initial developments of black theology. Cone celebrates that "they are breaking new theological ground, building on, challenging, and moving beyond the founders of black theology."[27]

Dwight N. Hopkins is a member of the group that Cone terms the "second generation" of black theologians. In *Introducing Black Theology of Liberation,* Hopkins clearly states that the dialogue between womanists and black theologians must continue:

> Womanist theologians and ethicists... have charted their own theological journey. They have challenged both the first and second generations of men theologians with issues of faith and practice which go as far back as the origin of black women in America, through the 1960s civil rights movement, up to today's African American church.[28]

Hopkins often works in collaboration with Linda Thomas, a womanist theologian, demonstrating his own commitment to continued dialogue. The two theologians also work together in international research among black South Africans. Both Cone's and Hopkins's perspectives indicate the importance of womanist thought in the development of black theology today.

In a larger framework, both womanist and black theology stand within the black faith traditions that bring theology to the locations where it is lived, in the pews, sacristies, and naves of churches. The resulting dialogue between womanist theologians and pastoral leaders often takes interesting twists.

Black Religious Traditions

> My great-grandmother, who could not read or write, used to love to hear talk about the Lord. She talked about the Lord as she would to a friend. I was always trying to find out, well, how do you get to be a friend to God like that?... and my great grandmother said, "Baby, let me tell you. If you ever

have anything to do with God, and if God ever had anything to do with you, he will not leave you a fool. You will
know."[29]

Black people have a history of finding strength in their religious lives, from hush arbors during enslavement to gospel music
today. Like the activist Jo Anne Watson, quoted above, religious
traditions inform the lives of many African Americans. For black
women, religiosity has shaped identity and becomes a legacy for
the next generation. The quote at the beginning of this section
points to black women as the source for understanding their
religious traditions. Denominations do not always shape this religiosity, but a faith formed by life is a key component.

Valerie E. James, an African American woman, describes God
in relation to gender:

> If there is a "he" God, I believe there is also a "she" God and
> a God for the people between the "hes" and the "shes." In
> other words, I do not envision a God who discriminates be-
> cause of gender or sexual preference. I envision a God of love
> for all creation. This includes the creation of the physical and
> non-physical, the visible and the invisible and all that which
> encompasses humankind.[30]

This author's ideas could be considered heretical within the
theological framework of many denominations. Womanist theologians can bring these ideas into churches and create new opportunities for dialogue. These ordinary theologies can energize
theological discussions, if they can be heard. To that end, womanists engaged in ministry encourage black women to speak up and
out. "You've thought it, but you held the thought inside. Either
there was no one to tell or no one cared. And besides, women who
point out problems are troublemakers."[31]

In addition to dialogue with black women in churches, womanist theologians also consider the structures of churches as sources
of empowerment of all the membership. Delores Williams identifies several complex issues. One set of those issues is the multiple
forms of sexist oppression (sexual and emotional exploitation, resistance to forms of ministry by and for women) experienced by

black women in some churches. Another set of issues focuses on
poor stewardship of human and monetary resources (building huge
church complexes when members are in poverty or the refusal to
address the social needs of parishioners or community).[32] None of
these issues is easily addressed and requires continued dialogue to
effect positive changes.

Another arena of concern is the daunting barriers encountered
by black women who attempt to go into professional ministry.
Katie Cannon, in a passage quoted earlier, has written powerfully
of the isolation of black women in seminary settings:

> As Black women pursuing advanced theological degrees,
> alienation, isolation, and marginalization were our daily fare.
> Even with the requisite credentials for matriculation in hand,
> we were constantly barraged with arrogance and insults, sus-
> picion and insensitivity, backhand compliments and tongue-
> in-cheek naiveté. The worlds of divinity school, denomina-
> tional headquarters, regional judicatory offices, and local
> parishes, between which we negotiated, demanded different
> and often wrenching allegiances. But we continued to study.[33]

Cheryl Townsend Gilkes, in her book *If It Wasn't for the
Women,* also deals with these issues and the contributions made
by black women:

> This book contains essays that place black women's agency,
> centrality, importance, and indispensability to their churches
> and communities in the foreground....I have concluded
> that black women are fundamentally correct in their self-
> assessment: "If it wasn't for the women," the black community
> would not have had the churches and other organizations that
> have fostered the psychic and material survival of individuals
> and that have mobilized the constituencies that have produced
> change and progress.[34]

Dialogue from and within black religious traditions — including
ordinary theologies, ministerial preparation, church life, and recognition of black women's importance — is critically important to the
continuing development of womanist theology.

Dialogue with Students:
Teaching Womanist Theology

A significant location of womanist dialogue has been the classroom. New ways of teaching and understanding theology occur as teacher and student become co-learners. The lines between the professional and the student are blurred but not erased. The classes become opportunities to explore the current realities of black women while resisting any reduction of those lives to single, essentialized categories. Questions are raised that test boundaries and are sometimes uncomfortable. Doing womanist theology is an interactive process, and the pedagogical processes that can be used in teaching womanist theology may threaten some students (and teachers), but liberate many others. A student once wept at the end of a class in womanist theology, grateful to learn that her religious questions were not "weird." She was then self-empowered to ask more questions.

Kelly Brown Douglas wrote of the challenges she faced as a teacher in developing a course in womanist theology. Without a model, she pulled together a course that was in a lecture format and consequently ineffective. This method does not create a community of learners. But, as Douglas considered the format, she wondered how a teacher could tap into the source of knowledge *within* the communities of black women. How could a teacher assist the students of any race or gender or class to honor their own wisdom? To enter this territory is to walk on risky pedagogical ground: the teacher risks control, distance, and the safety that comes from being emotionally detached.

Douglas experimented and found several components for an effective womanist pedagogy. First, students must dialogue with black women's history and come to recognize historical role models. Ideally, students should dialogue with black women outside the academic community and not limit their conversation partners. In addition, Douglas affirms that understanding the range of diversity among black women is critical to womanist theology. "Only after gaining some familiarity with what it means to be black and female can students critically reflect upon black women's theological concerns and affirmations."[35] Students must also dialogue with each

other, which becomes a form of networking and community building that promotes respect among scholars. Douglas concludes: "The
most important and enduring essential for womanist pedagogy is
flexibility. A womanist pedagogy must allow for change so as to
embrace the complex and dynamic reality of black womanhood."[36]

Katie Cannon presents another model of womanist pedagogy
that grew from the challenges she encountered teaching womanist ideas in seminary settings. Using as a metaphor the vision of
the biblical Ezekiel — wheels in the middle of wheels — Cannon
envisions womanist pedagogy as a form of resistance to narrow
perspectives of seminary education. By the structure of classes and
the emphases of faculty, seminary education often effects erasure or
diminution of black women's religious validity in fields of theology
or ethics. Womanist resistance is needed in such settings as a way
of encountering the truths of black women's lives. The three wheels
in Cannon's pedagogical image are the intellectual traditions of the
North Atlantic, the complex realities of African Christianity, and
black women's experiences.[37]

While womanist theology is not just for black women, there
is a special liberative focus in communicating with black women.
Sheron C. Patterson's *New Faith* is an example of a book written
to communicate womanist thought to black Christian women. Patterson invites her readers to enter the processes: "New Faith gives
us the chance to start from scratch, name our goals, name our God
in our language, speak our faith in our terms. To do all of this, we
must move counter-culture [*sic*]. Let's move."[38] Womanist dialogue
with students intentionally seeks to move them to define and act
on their faith beliefs.

Womanist Thought in the Diaspora: Global Dialogue

Black people are spread throughout the globe: in Belize, Haiti,
Canada, the United States, Europe, and the countries of Africa. The
term "African Diaspora" is used to discuss black people around the
world who were dispersed by force or choice from the continent
of Africa; it also includes those still on the continent. The variety

of black people in multiple countries, with different customs and languages, throughout the Diaspora makes for rich conversations.

Black women in the Diaspora have many conversations and connections to discover. What gender role expectations are placed on black women in Cuba? Do black women in Brazil experience racism? What are the class distinctions affecting black women in Senegal? How do these social constructions affect the religious lives of the women? What are the distinct or unique components of their lives? Answers of women in their respective countries will enable richer conversations among black women, for the range of expressions may provide points of similarity and distinction.

More and more women are answering such questions. Religious conversations were particularly aided by certain events of the 1970s. Ursula King pinpointed the World Council of Churches' 1974 consultation titled "Sexism in the 1970s" and the United Nations declaration of 1975–85 as the "Decade of Women" as instrumental. In 1976, the Ecumenical Association of Third World[39] Theologians (EATWOT) held its first meeting. As King noted, women were not involved in the first meetings, but "they soon came to represent a third of its membership."[40]

Several African women's perspectives are included in King's collection of Third World feminist theology. Some common themes surfaced. Bettye Ekeya of the Iteso in Uganda stated: "One section of these people remains poor, captive, blind, downtrodden, and unaware that the Lord's favor rests upon them. This group is African women."[41] Grace Eneme of the Bakossi people in southwest Cameroon wrote: "For decades we have been taught to be subordinate, 'little angels,' and all the way through those social tapes play back to us. In the family we are subordinate. In the church we are subordinate. In the offices, despite the laws and decrees made by the state to ensure equality, we are subordinate."[42] Mercy Amba Oduyoye is from the Akan people of the Ivory Coast and Ghana. The Akan are matrilineal, so Oduyoye brings a different perspective, which is much less patriarchal. However, as she moved outside the Akan, she states, "I have had problems with how the Church, academia, and the patriarchal society into which I married assign roles to women. My definition of personhood and identity as an Akan has led me several times into conflicts with role-expectations of people around me."[43]

The themes that surface in these writings have some connecting points, as pointed out by Virginia Fabella:

> The work of reformulating theology from the perspective of Third World women entails both reworking classical themes such as christology and ecclesiology, as well as reflecting on current concerns, such as the growing violence against women and the ecosystem.... They do theology with "passion and compassion," which they may express in poetry and song.... Life is central and women affirm their solidarity with all who struggle for life.[44]

These themes are reminiscent of those raised in womanist theology. Future conversations will assist in creating distinctions among the different women of the Diaspora as well as finding new links.

Discussion Questions

1. What are the most important issues for black communities in the United States? Are you familiar with an Afrocentric solution to this issue? If there is such a solution, would womanists agree or disagree? On what do you base your argument?

2. Define some differences between black feminists and womanists. What are some of the differences between womanists and white feminists? Which of the differences can become talking points for dialogue?

3. Teaching womanist theology usually aims for "co-learning" between teachers and students. Do you think this is possible? Have you ever been in such a collaborative educational effort? Did it work? Why or why not?

4. From a recent newspaper, identify one situation in need of the attention of a faith community. What is important about your selection? Which faith community would best address the situation? What are some of the considerations to be addressed? (This is an exercise that begins "doing" theology.)

5. Does one have to be a womanist to teach womanist theology?

Chapter 6

Womanist Theology, Constructed

This chapter examines specific constructions of womanist theology. There are several themes that have flowed easily from the signal texts that were discussed in chapter 4. Beginning with Jacquelyn Grant's questions about christology, womanist theologians have explored the shape of black women's suffering, the meanings of salvation and christology, and understandings of God and the Bible. Each of these theological constructions is centered on underlying understandings of the humanness of black women.

These topics — salvation, christology, and so on — are considered foundational of all theologies. The topics respond to the deepest questions of human explorations in faith. Who is God? What is the faith community? Who is the human person? How are these related? The answers that womanists find are not always in accord with those of white, Western, or male theologies because black women's lives have shaped other meanings. This chapter briefly considers some of the more established constructions of womanist theology. These are not closed, absolute, or hardened constructions; womanists continue to explore each of the categories. Yet these are noted because of the amount of work that has already been invested in dialogue about them.

The principles of womanist theology that were outlined in chapter 3 are:

- Womanist theology is focused on black women, analyzing the intricate layers of their lives. This focus aims to uncover the ordinary theologies that operate within black women's

105

lives and incorporate these ideas in womanist theological constructions.

- The communal dimensions of black women's experiences often inform the ordinary theologies, especially those regarding family life and social activism. These dimensions take many forms, including that of networking among black women.

- The scope of womanist theology demands the creative use of multidisciplinary methodologies.

- Ethical and social analyses of all forms of oppressions give definition to womanist theology.

- Ongoing dialogues with other perspectives are constitutive of constructions of womanist theology. The dialogues take on particular intensity when internal to the intellectual traditions of the black communities.

Suffering and Salvation

Discussion of salvation, a central tenet of Christianity, will always raise questions for oppressed people. In the lives of black women, the tridimensional oppressions of race, class, and gender have shaped daily life. These experiences of oppression would seemingly cripple or destroy the human person. Yet, in the face of these experiences, black women continue to have faith in a saving God. What does salvation mean in such a context? Does salvation erase suffering? Or are pain and loss "good" for a person? Is salvation oxymoronic for suffering women?

The agenda laid out by Jacquelyn Grant in *White Women's Christ, Black Women's Jesus* provides direction. Grant calls for close scrutiny of African American women's experiences of oppression in all its forms; a focus on new ways of theologically defining and understanding Christ; and the development of a holistic christology.[1] Christology is Christianity's central doctrine, for defining Jesus as Lord and Messiah is not merely a historic claim, but must be clarified for each succeeding generation of believers. Yet asking how African American women can claim Jesus as Savior in the midst of assorted, interwoven oppressions is a powerful question. The simplest answer, of course, is that black women seek a way to deny pain, to create an imaginary world for escapism, or to imagine a reward for that suffering. But there are no easy answers, for the experiences of oppression in relation to religion are complex.

As Jacquelyn Grant continues her investigations of salvation and christology, she situates the meanings of sadness and sorrow in black women's lives, drawing a frame of reference from a choreopoem of the playwright Ntozake Shange:

> In the experiences of Black women, Jesus was ever-present; he has commonly been perceived as present in "times of trouble." Ntozake Shange ... commented through one of her characters that to speak of Black women's existence as "colored and sorry" is to be redundant. Sadness or sorrow (the pain, the sufferings) are perpetually a part of the African American woman's reality; so much so that, whatever else the consideration, these components are always present in the lives of Black women. Consequently, to be "colored and sorry" is to be redundant.[2]

The reality of suffering must be part of the analysis of black women's understandings of salvation: Jesus is present *in* the troubles. Analysis of suffering is not enough however. Grant is careful to include the tradition of black women's self-liberatory actions within her explorations. In other words, not only the sadness, but also the grace-filled transforming moments must be recognized as components of the whole understanding of salvation. Grant utilizes the words and actions of black women in history to make this point. Sojourner Truth is one example that Grant presents. A recorded sermon by Truth tells of "her encounter with Jesus [that] brought such joy that she became overwhelmed with love and praise.... This love is not a sentimental, passive love. It was a tough, active love that empowered her to fight more fiercely for the freedom of her people."[3]

Theologian M. Shawn Copeland views suffering as a point from which to develop womanist theology. Elegantly drawing on black women's experiences of pain, she cites a saying of Gullah women, "Ah done been in sorrow's kitchen and ah licked de pots clean." Suffering, in Copeland's view, is any mental, emotional, spiritual, or physical force that radically disrupts lives. "Evil is the negation and deprivation of good; suffering, while never identical with evil, is inseparable from it."[4] Black women's historically conditioned sources of resisting suffering include the *memory* of past injustices as well as actions to create a self-defined future; *language,* especially sass, which is audacious, bold, and willful words that guard identity; and *religion,* the Christianity shaped by African values, oppressed conditions, and, based on these, interaction with biblical texts.[5] Ultimately then, a womanist theology of suffering is redemptive as "Black women invite God to partner them in the redemption of Black people."[6]

There are connections between the historical "suffering" of black women and experiences of "suffering" today, including the imprisonment of black women in poverty, low wages, and domestic violence; and dangers from HIV/AIDS, breast cancer, poor nutrition, and continued social invisibility. Cheryl A. Kirk-Duggan connects the music of black women, specifically blues and gospel artists, with salvific actions. She states that musical artists

> call everyone to (1) be real; (2) name the oppressions . . . and work to transcend them; (3) celebrate ourselves, our gifts, and each other; (4) recognize the Blues and deal with them; (5) recognize the Gospel message and live by it; and (6) live life and do your job with integrity. . . . One is justified and saved to be loved: doing love better and living life rightly. . . . One is redeemed and freed toward greatness and community.[7]

Womanist considerations of salvation are not exercises in academic abstractions but name black women's meanings, give grounds for resistance, and are intended for the use of the community.

Analyses of suffering or pain springing from socially constructed racial, gender, or class categories are necessary constituents of any theological construction of salvation that relates to black women. Explorations of the possible meanings of this suffering never grant some state of goodness to experiences of oppression. Instead, the various responses to pain highlight the agency of black women, who seek ways to create their own good. Agency, discussed in general in the first chapter, becomes a pivotal principle in comprehending black women's concepts of salvation. Through agency (the ability of a person or community to work on their own behalf, within or in spite of existing social institutions), they are able to create new realities in order to resist dehumanization. M. Shawn Copeland's discussion of developing a black women's theology of suffering, characterized by resistance through "sass," communal memories, and religious traditions, makes sense in this view.

Suffering in itself is not salvific. It is redemptive only in that it may lead to critical rethinking of meaning or purpose, as might any life crisis. Such reexamination is part of the process of human maturation. However, suffering is a distinctive starting place for thinking about salvation as it brings into sharp focus human experience in relation to God.

For other theologies, the acts of the individual person become an important point for a journey toward salvation, particularly through a personal choice to separate from the evil knowingly committed. Issues of personal responsibility have been stressed in North Atlantic traditions, particularly in the United States with its neon-lit ethos of the rugged individual. This view easily turns to individualism, with its inability to recognize the social dimensions of sin or the communal responsibilities of faith. In some pastoral settings, the concept of sin masks sexism and is used to control women's activities and roles within churches. The negative impact of this oppression is multiplied in those black churches where racism is intertwined with sexism: women may be bound by denominational restrictions, but the real sin is sin against them.[8]

Womanist theology invites black women to step away from these ideas and to reconsider meanings from their own perspectives. "I am a womanist because I boldly look through my own eyes and see Jesus for myself.... You will discover as I did there is more to God. And if we are to experience it, we must stop waiting on someone to spoon-feed us. Let's seize it."[9] This call stands as a liberative theme within womanist theological constructions. Womanist theology, by beginning with black women's suffering, reconfigures doctrinal themes related to salvation, including sin, community, and responsibility.

The notion of sin, so important in most Christian constructions of salvation, takes on a different cast in black women's
understandings. These understandings are grounded in those of the
African American community's religious thought. Delores Williams
draws from the history of African Americans and locates historical sources for considering sin. In each, she identifies a sense of
sin that is unlike that of Western thought. Two of those sources
are the spiritual songs and the autobiographies of former slaves.
In these, sin is related to troubles. Those who oppress are deemed
evil in both sources. There is an understanding of personal evil,
but also "there is that transgression that involves collective social
evil."[10] Social sin, which is committed through structures such as
slavery, is recognized, and damnation is the expected punishment
from God.

For Williams, a womanist construction of sin has several characteristics. The first is that, because humans are created in God's
image, any abuse or defilement of the body is sin. For black
women, abuse has occurred through the elevation of white womanhood and the devaluation of black womanhood. Abuse was
perpetrated on black women through the legal system's indifference
to "the defilement of Black women's bodies — especially through
overwork, lynching, and rape of Black women by white men."[11]
Therefore, she contends, "to devalue the womanhood and sexuality of Black women is sin; to devalue the womanhood and sexuality
of Black lesbian women is also sin;...the womanist notion of sin
in this essay takes seriously Black women's depleted self-esteem."[12]
Salvation, from this view, entails "elevating and healing Black
women's self-esteem."[13]

Jacquelyn Grant has developed an understanding of sin that
focuses on the need to elevate black women's self-esteem. She analyzes the concept of servanthood, another social ideology that was
and is used to keep black women in place. Servanthood, in the
negative sense, slipped into an interpretation of meek submission
to the dominant group. This type of servanthood became wed-
ded to theological constructions that oppressed black women. With
this in mind, Grant could ask, "What sense does it make to re-
joice in the service of a man (Jesus), who has been used not to
save but to exploit?"[14] In this view, the labor of black women

is constantly devalued. So where is salvation? African American women "could go to church on Tuesday, Wednesday nights and Sunday morning and testify to being a better servant of the Lord and Savior Jesus."[15] For black women, sin is too much service, for it has invited them to self-destructive behaviors. In contrast, Grant posits the concept of discipleship. "Women must be empowered to become disciples. The language of discipleship for women provides the possibility of breaking down traditional stereotypical, exclusivistic understandings of discipleship."[16]

These ideas of sin broaden the discussion of salvation already presented. A womanist statement of salvation must reflect black women's lives, consistent with the textures of their daily experiences and ordinary theologies. Faith in Jesus should empower black women to wholeness, not self-destruction. Delores Williams has made one of the most definitive statements of salvation and its meaning for black women:

> The resurrection of Jesus and the kingdom of God theme in Jesus' *ministerial* vision provide black women with the knowledge that God has, through Jesus, shown humankind how to live peacefully, productively and abundantly in relationship. Jesus showed humankind a vision of righting relations between body, mind and spirit.[17]

Williams uses black women's experiences to express one meaning of redemption. (Implications of Williams's assertion of the centrality of Jesus' ministerial vision will be discussed in more detail in the next section.) Her construction dually honors black women's experiences of suffering from various oppressions, as well as ordinary theologies that find salvation in Jesus. Salvation, then, in a womanist construction, is not found in formulaic answers but in the search for wholeness. Redemption is a journey that begins by daring to care for self in the face of repeated assaults on identity and value. Salvation is born of the struggle to reconcile some assigned "place" in the world with a self-determined identity that springs from hope and is grounded in faith.

Williams's consideration of right relationships leads to other aspects of salvation: community and social responsibility. Salvation in a womanist view desires transformation of self *and* society.

Studies of black women's spiritual biographies serve to point to these themes. For example, Septima Clark, who is considered the mother of the Civil Rights Movement, stated her motivations for dealing with the dangers of working with the Southern Christian Leadership Council's Citizen Education Project:

> The way I see it, the test is on us now, those who believe in nonviolence and brotherhood. Things which I hear labeled out-of-date and unrealistic, we must make work. We must build a foundation, through the long hot summers and long cold winters. This foundation, whether rooted in Christianity or single person-to-person contact, must achieve what has not been done before, and it must be solidly rooted in truth and love.[18]

When African American women have reexamined their lives following pain, a response has often been greater dedication to the life of the community, to networking, to working for others. Salvation becomes a community event. As has happened repeatedly in the lives of black women, from Ida Wells Barnett to Fannie Lou Hamer, activism for the greater community is birthed. Each person is saved not merely for self, but for community. A person is saved *from* socially structured limitations, saved *for* the greater good of all people.

Jacquelyn Grant gives another example of this call for the greater community, based on the experiences of Harriet Tubman. When Tubman realized that her escape from slavery was successful and she was finally free, she likened her freedom to being in heaven. However, the realization dawned that she had left behind her family, the old folks, and others in the bonds of slavery. She determined to bring them to freedom as well. In Tubman's words, "Oh, how I prayed then, lying all alone on the cold, damp ground: 'Oh, dear Lord...I ain't got no friend but you. Come to my help, Lord, for I'm in trouble!' "[19] Grant highlights that Tubman's freedom was "trouble" that had to be shared; like the gospel song, Tubman "just couldn't keep it to herself." In setting her course of action, Tubman would move into conflict with the status quo and with the laws and customs of the land.

Delores Williams has further explored the ideas of righting relationships by calling for the wholeness of all African American
people, with the Civil Rights Movement as model.[20] Thinking of
a "resurrection of the Black civil rights movement" as a necessity
for the black community, she has advocated for social salvation
through the leadership of churches, especially in regard to peace-
making in all relationships. "There can be no holiness, no unity
and no catholicity of the Christian church until it identifies itself in
active opposition to all forms of violence against humans (female
and male), against nature (including nonhuman animals), against
the environment and against the land."[21]

Womanist doctrinal explorations, Williams affirms, are bonded
to explorations of the experiences of black women, the needs of the
black communities, and activism on behalf of both. The womanist constructions of salvation, with related discussions of suffering,
are but beginning points in the larger project that Jacquelyn Grant
defines: development of a holistic womanist christology.

Reconsidering Christology

Salvation and suffering provide a rich field for the continued doctrinal exploration of christology from black women's perspectives.
The preceding discussions already surfaced questions of Jesus being the Savior for black women. Jacquelyn Grant, Kelly Brown
Douglas, and Delores Williams are particularly significant in their
explorations of christological questions.

Jacquelyn Grant has offered some of the most thorough analyses of black women's understandings of Jesus. She grounds her
discussion in the historical African American religious community,
where Jesus was a primary frame of reference who was viewed
as the "divine co-sufferer." "As Jesus was persecuted and made
to suffer undeservedly, so were they. His suffering culminated in
the crucifixion. Their crucifixion included rapes, and husbands being castrated (literally and metaphorically), babies being sold, and
other cruel and often murderous treatments."[22]

Grant contends that this Jesus, seen from black women's experientially based views, is liberated by black women, as he liberates

them. Jesus is liberated from his historical imprisonment by controlling patriarchy, white supremacist ideology, and the privileged class. In addition to the liberating image of co-sufferer, Jesus is seen by black women as equalizer since he is for all people regardless of class, race, caste, or gender. Jesus is seen as freedom because he challenges each believer to move past mere equality as a goal for justice into the goal of full liberation for all. Jesus is the sustainer for people in great need. Jesus is the liberator who empowers black women to work for the liberation of others.[23]

Kelly Brown Douglas, a womanist theologian, explores the shape of christology primarily from the perspective of the black community in her book *The Black Christ*.[24] In the social justice struggles of the 1960s, black Americans "needed to know, in no uncertain terms, if Jesus Christ was for or against them. There was no room for ambiguity. Either Jesus supported their struggle for respect and freedom, or he did not. At stake was the integrity of Black people's Christian identity."[25] From this vantage point, Douglas scrutinizes the christological constructions of both black and feminist theologies and cites the shortfalls of both in addressing the religious needs of African American women. The concept of a black Christ arose from constructions of black male theologians. Womanist theology, which aims to speak to and from black women's realities, reaches a different christological statement. In addition to considering a black Christ, womanists focus on Jesus as integral to African American communities — to their people and their struggles for wholeness. Douglas defines a womanist black Christ as present in the social justice struggles of black people and as imaged in the heroines and heroes of those struggles. Christ must be seen in the "faces of the poorest black women, . . . [who are] reminders of accountability."[26]

Douglas also analyzes the implications of these realities for doctrinal constructions, especially as regards the Nicene or Apostles' Creed. For many Christian traditions, either creed is a definitive statement of Jesus as Christ. Douglas points out that something important is missing that womanists wish to avoid:

> There are aspects of the Nicene/Chalcedonian formulation that appear inconsistent with Jesus as he was presented in

the Gospels. For instance, this formulation establishes that Jesus is Christ by focusing on God's act of becoming incarnate in him. In so doing, it diminishes the significance of Jesus' actions on earth. His ministry is virtually ignored.[27]

The image of Jesus as co-sufferer who is involved in mutual liberation with black women resonates with the central place his ministry is given in these christological constructions. Recovering Jesus' ministry as central to understanding his meaning in the lives of his followers is a catalyst for theological reflection. The Nicene tradition, Douglas charges, ignores Jesus' ministry. Womanists are certainly "doing" christology because they are exploring the meanings of Jesus Christ for themselves, using the base of black religious traditions. However, Douglas states, womanists are not doing christology if it "means that the Nicene/Chalcedonian tradition must provide a norm or even a significant source for what we say about Jesus as Christ."[28]

Delores Williams's concept of Jesus' ministerial vision figures prominently in her christological construction, which is challenging on several levels as she revisits Jesus' importance to black women. Jesus' vision is found in his life actions, not his death. By rethinking the location of Jesus' vision, Williams points black women toward rethinking the importance of their own lives. It is not suffering or surrogacy or defilement that "saves":

> Humankind is, then, redeemed through Jesus' *ministerial* vision of life and not through his death. There is nothing divine in the blood of the cross. God does not intend black women's surrogacy experience. Neither can Christian faith affirm such an idea. Jesus did not come to be a surrogate. Jesus came for life, to show humans a perfect vision of ministerial relation that humans had very little knowledge of. As Christians, black women cannot forget the cross, but neither can they glorify it.[29]

The ministries of this vision include faith and prayer, words and touch, exorcising evil, and compassion and love. With this view, Jesus' resurrection was triumphal not because of the brutality of crucifixion, but because that ministerial vision was incapable of being destroyed by human evil. Williams separates black women's understanding of Jesus from the crucifixion because of the history of black women's suffering. That suffering took on the particular cast of black women's surrogacy, which was forced upon them under the centuries of enslavement and was seemingly voluntary in the following centuries. Both types of surrogacy highlight the use that has been made of black women by American society. With this in mind, Williams challenges any view of Jesus, for African American women, that is bound by the idea of atonement for sin by suffering. Otherwise, she contends, black women are only giving glory to their own surrogacy. Therefore, it follows that being a Christian involves participation in Jesus' ministerial vision, rather than meekly suffering oppressions.

In light of this ministerial vision, Williams reconsiders the meaning of Jesus' birth, the incarnation. Jesus becoming human should "be regarded as a continuum of the manifestation of divine spirit beginning with Mary, becoming an abundance in Jesus and later overflowing into the life of the church."[30] The role of women in birthing new realities through openness to the Spirit is informed by Jesus' incarnation, which becomes a possibility for each generation.

These christological conversations are sometimes uncomfortable and controversial. Is faith supposed to be a matter of comfort or safety? Is the theological task bound up with keeping people wrapped in cotton batting? Faith is a divine gift understood through human activities of belief, trust, action, and doubt. If a theology reflects on all these components from the perspective of the human community, then unsettling questions, instead of neatly packaged answers, must result. This is to say that womanists do not view their theological constructions as hardened into dogma, but are committed to continued discussion of God's presence in daily life. JoAnne Marie Terrell is a womanist theologian whose study of christology leads to other conclusions.[31]

Terrell challenges Williams's decentering of Jesus' cross based upon the lives and beliefs of African American women. There is value in the concept of the cross and in the idea of the black community's sacrifice. Terrell states that these ideas "got lost in the rhetorical impetus of [Williams's] language of surrogacy."[32]

Instead, the idea of Jesus suffering invites those who live in oppression to identify with God's love:

> I believe that Christians need to ponder the implications of Christ's death continuously, because the drama testifies to the exceedingly great lengths to which God goes to advise the extent of human estrangement. It is no slight on the intelligence of black women when they confess this; rather, it reflects on what they say they need and what they say Christ's real presence, mediated through the gospel, provides — redemption and release from the self-alienation and social alienation they experience in their workaday lives.[33]

A Word about Womanist Biblical Scholarship

The Bible has been very important in the construction of womanist theology because of its importance in the lives of black women. Jacquelyn Grant contends that African American women claim two sources of revelation: the Bible and the wisdom born from their personal relationships with God. Both sources became lenses through which to analyze their experience. "The understanding of God as creator, sustainer, comforter, and liberator took on life as they agonized over their pain, and celebrated the hope that as God delivered the Israelites, they would be delivered as well."[34] Biblical references and connections are constantly made in the ordinary theologies of black women.

Delores Williams and Renita Weems both use the biblical tale of Hagar as a source of reflection. This use is reflective of already existing strands of black women's thinking. Williams demonstrates these interpretive connections to the black community in her comments on the "Universal Hagar's Spiritual Church."[35] This is but one indication that there is something distinctive about the womanist use of scripture. Williams maintains that, like feminists, womanists utilize a hermeneutical posture of suspicion, carefully sorting through the subtexts of scriptural writings and interpretations. Womanists also should have a hermeneutical posture of affirmation, which uses African American women's understandings and traditions as reference points.[36] These ideas reflect Grant's idea of black women's experiences as a source of wisdom in connection with scripture.

Despite these uses and the contributions of womanists such as Renita Weems, some difficulties remain with the state of biblical scholarship. On one level, there are few black women who specialize in the field of biblical scholarship. In a survey (2000), Randall C. Bailey listed forty-five African Americans with doctoral degrees in biblical studies. Of these, only eleven are women.[37] This lack of presence of black women indicates two things. First, there is a need for more black people, men and women, in biblical studies generally. Second, when more black women are involved in that theological discipline, it will be possible to more fully express black women's biblical interpretations.

Another issue is raised by the state of biblical scholarship among black scholars. Vincent L. Wimbush, a black theologian, has called for a reconsideration of biblical studies in relation to the black community. His revolutionary look at the Bible recognizes that there is a need for "an openness to beginning the study of the Bible (as it were) in a different key — *in a different time*, which means from a *different site of interpretation and enunciation*, with the necessarily correlative *presuppositions, orientations and agenda*."[38] He is currently working with groups of scholars and students at Union Theological Seminary in New York City to explore the meaning of the Bible from the perspectives of the black community.

Both the increase in the number of black women in biblical scholarship and the impetus of Wimbush's questions will strengthen existing statements of womanist theology. Exploring black women's unique interpretations or hermeneutics of scripture will most likely lead to new expressions of womanist theologies. The area of womanist biblical scholarship has great promise.

Questions of God

Integral to Christianity is the idea of the Trinity of God, the three persons of Parent, Son Jesus, and Holy Spirit. As womanists have reconsidered christological constructions, have new questions about God arisen? Diana Hayes, Karen Baker-Fletcher, and Cheryl Kirk-Duggan provide considerations.

Diana Hayes provides the historic grounding when she considers the ordinary theologies of God found in African Americans' religious thought:

> God was a warrior God whose intervention led to their freedom as a result of the Civil War; God was a just God who did not abide the sins of their masters for long; God was a saving and liberating God whose promise of salvation was both personal (spiritual) and communitarian (physical) for all who believed and maintained their faith, but God was also a loving mother who nurtured and sustained her children in their struggle.[39]

Hayes's words state the context that informs womanist theologians' reflections on God. This sustaining, warring, saving God is known through scriptural reflections and personal experiences. The scriptural reflections are responses to questions about God's reality for people who are oppressed. The personal experiences are reflected in hundreds of writings by black people, from autobiographies of ex-slaves[40] to contemporary confessional-style memoirs.[41]

Karen Baker-Fletcher draws from the ordinary theologies of black women to name a womanist theology of God. God is both "strength of life" and "empowering Spirit." These understandings of God are directly related to black women's experiences of oppression. "God is neither simply the ultimate ground of being by which we are grasped in moments of mystical experience nor some ultimate point of reference whom we come to understand primarily by reason. It is in our human bodies."[42] Baker-Fletcher asserts that black women experience God as immanent and embodied. In this womanist view, God continues to reveal God's Self in daily life. God's self-revelation is not for personal self-gratification but, instead, calls the faithful person to be for the good of the community. "To work for the healing and wholeness of community is to act in harmony with God, who as the strength of life is the source of healing and wholeness."[43]

Baker-Fletcher also discusses the necessity of recognizing that human knowledge is limited, so all theological constructions are ongoing projects. "Admitting that our knowledge of God is not a finished product but limited in scope is the first step toward non-idolatrous imaging of God. It reminds us that imaging God is the most humble, finite of tasks."[44] In like manner, she warns against the limits of faith in denominations. Churches are human institutions that do not *cause* faith in God. "Ultimately, however, faith in God must emerge from something deeper and more ancient, . . . the divine ground of all creation, of all that is and all that will be — God Godself."[45]

Cheryl Kirk-Duggan's womanist writing analyzes human violence. She charges that such a task is a necessity for those who claim to be believers in a loving Divine Being. By questioning the continued existence of violence in our world, Kirk-Duggan brings the historical questions of the enslaved to the modern world: How can we believe in a loving God in the face of continued evil? "When we destroy nature and that which makes us human, we betray God and all of humanity."[46] The immanence of God is clear in her construction, for *we* have the potential to betray God with nature-destroying activities. God is fully present in our lives, and we are called to be responsible and care for each other. Kirk-Duggan offers womanist theory as a method for a corrective analysis. "Womanist theory embodies a Refiner's Fire: God's powerful grace lived out in humanity toward transformation. In the crucible of life, this Refiner's Fire can assist us in addressing issues related to women, humanity, religion and violence. Womanist theory refines our seeing, thinking, hearing, and living."[47] Womanist theoretical activity is aligned with God's purposes and aims to continue radically considering liberative possibilities for all humans.

These constructions are continuing. For example, the sense of the Spirit, the Holy Ghost, is prominent in the everyday lives of black women and needs further womanist exploration. The concept of the Trinity is currently being explored in the work of Sister Jamie Phelps, O.P. Concern for gendered God-language has historically figured less prominently in the lives of black women in churches.[48] That silence is being rightly shattered as black women are invited to consider the power of their words: "As quiet as it is kept, God is more than a father; God is also a midwife.... My favorite image is of God as a mother hen, fiercely protective and efficient.... Sisters, I believe that the use of inclusive language gives our relationships with God, ourselves, and others a sane foundation."[49] These words are invitations to deeper reflection on God's and black women's identities. The God-centered humanity of black women is an ongoing exploration of womanist theologians.

Personhood

> To be a Black woman in today's world is to be an anomaly of sorts. It is, on the one hand, to be treated as someone who has performed miracles simply by continuing to persist in living life as she and she alone sees fit. On the other hand, it is to be narrowly watched, critiqued and judged for every action, every step, almost every breath taken.... Claiming and proclaiming one's voice as a Black woman, especially in today's Christian church, both Black and white, is an enterprise fraught with perils.[50]

Diana Hayes's words capture the struggle of learning to live as black women in American society. Her words recenter the context of the preceding sections on womanist theological constructions. African American women have struggled in the processes of identifying who they are in the eyes of God as they stand against misrepresentation and stereotype. The naming process is the work of Christian anthropology, which is foundational for any theology. Returning to the principles outlined at the beginning of the chapter, womanist theologians have looked to the lives of black women as primary sources for these self-defined understandings.

Karen Baker-Fletcher has focused on the work of Anna Julia Cooper, a nineteenth-century black woman, and found that "great women of the past and the present, along with their communities, offer important information about the possibilities of becoming, of moving into fuller realization or development of human potential."[51] Baker-Fletcher has utilized Cooper's life as a major resource in her work to identify black women's "gifts of power for survival and wholeness," which are generative powers developed in response to oppression. She names five generative powers: the power of voice, the power of making do, the power of memory, the power of holding things together, and the power of generation.[52] The power of voice names experience, community, God, and self. Voice creates rather than accepts identity, and ultimately leads to the call for reform. The power of "making do" resonates with Delores Williams's concept of survival and quality of life, by which black women creatively shape lives. "In the midst of scarcity, this ethic functions as a power of material survival and spiritual thriving. In the midst of abundance, it works as a power of material and spiritual thriving."[53] The power of remembering involves more than a memory of ancestors' glory and pain; it is also a recognition of the aspects of self, whether success or failure, that might be denied. This full acceptance of self is liberating. The power of holding things together is the determined preservation of "life, family, and community." Baker-Fletcher describes the power of generation in relationship to womanist thought: "Womanists are Black women who pass on the gift of holding things together from generation to generation." The power of generation is deemed "vital to the renewed existence of faith communities."[54] Baker-Fletcher's concepts reconfigure the way that womanists consider the history, life, and creative impulses of black women.

In her work to understand these generative powers, Baker-Fletcher constructs a womanist Christian anthropology. She does not attempt to make these powers universal for all human beings, yet they are fully human experiences to which other people can relate. "Such embodiment reflects creation in God's likeness among Black women and anyone else who embodies these generative powers."[55] The humanity of black women is aligned with that of others, as expressions of God's creation. The statements of the personhood of black women and the definition of the meanings of their humanity confirm black women's self-perceptions. But this is not just a humanistic exercise; a Christian anthropology must encompass the meanings of faith.

The meaning of Christian life revolves around faith. Womanist understandings of faith in a nurturing God, Jesus of the ministerial vision, and a Spirit of empowerment are woven into the meaning of

life. These beliefs are invitations not into passivity but into action
for justice for the life of the community. Diana Hayes notes that an
active faith can move mountains:

> We must live our lives, both publicly and privately, in the
> same subversive manner that Jesus Christ led his. For our
> God *is* a God who takes sides, the side of those most in
> need....To subvert means to turn reality upside down, to
> look at it in another light, to confound those who believe
> they are the only source of truth by presenting another, more
> far-reaching and earth-shattering truth.[56]

Linking faith in a God who takes the side of those most in need
with the generative powers of black women is a creative process.
Delving into the humanity of black women must include suffering,
which becomes a window for reimagining God. Looking into the
faith of African American women leads back to a reconsideration
of the depths of their humanity. Within such contexts, womanist
theology is constructed.

Discussion Questions

1. What does it mean to be human?

2. Define what faith means to you? How have you come to
   believe this?

3. Describe salvation from a womanist perspective.

4. Define who God (by any name) is to you? How did you come
   to this realization? Has it changed over the years?

Chapter 7

New Challenges, Lingering Questions

In the process of constructing black women's theologies, different perspectives on themes such as salvation and christology enrich the dialogue. While these are significant areas that need further exploration, the work of womanist theologians is not restricted to these areas. This chapter will consider some of the newer themes that womanists have begun to discuss. These include pastoral theology, ecumenical dialogue, traditional African religion, sexuality, and ethnography and art.

Pastoral Theology

Pastoral theology, also called "practical" theology, is sometimes viewed as less important than theoretical constructions. However, womanist theology is serious about ensuring that practice and theory are connected: as we say, not merely God-*talk*, but God-*walk*. Many womanist theologians and ethicists are also practitioners, some involved in preaching, in ministry groups, and in the formation of other ministers.

This connection between theory and practice has a healing dimension, whether in educational institutions, the community, or the marketplace. Womanist theologians, if serious about speaking the truth of black women's lives, must necessarily remain connected to the wider community. Teresa Fry Brown delivers a stinging reminder to womanist scholars:

> There are womanist scholars who are active in local churches, drawing strength from everyday, ordinary sisters. However,

there are also scholars who have wrapped themselves in the robes of ivory-tower elitism and do not deal with Black women's daily reality unless one of our colleagues unceremoniously reminds us that we are still Black women in America.[1]

Brown drew her model from her work over a number of years with a church-based group of black women in Denver: Sisters Working Encouraging Empowering Together, or S.W.E.E.T. The story of S.W.E.E.T. is reminiscent of the Detroit Metropolitan Black Women's Health Project: both aim for the healing and self-esteem of African American women. A significant difference is that participants in S.W.E.E.T. are more deliberately church-centered. Their networking demonstrates that healing work with black women is possible in churches, but that a broader and more systematic approach is needed. The links between theory and practice will happen when black women in the academy work with those in churches to positively impact pastoral theology. Marsha Foster Boyd, Carroll Watkins Ali, and Cheryl Kirk-Duggan are three womanist theologians involved in creating these pastoral connections.

Marsha Foster Boyd reports on a group of black women ministers, social workers, pastors, and professors who have formed a group called WomanistCare.[2] This approach is different from the shepherd/flock model of ministry, which is deemed white and male, as well as the model of the "wounded healer," which is deemed crippling. Defining the WomanistCare approach, Boyd writes:

> WomanistCare is the intentional process of care giving and receiving by African American women. It is the African American woman finding her place and her voice in this world. It is the bold expression of that woman caring for her circle.... The focus is the holistic care of body, mind, and spirit in order that healing and transformation occur for African American women and their circles of influence.[3]

Boyd envisions ministry as a collaborative project, coining the term "empowered cojourner" as a way to understand the companionship and conversation that occur among the ministerial circle. WomanistCare has several components. The first is communication, with special attention to listening. Second is the affirmation of African American women's dreams, narratives, and feelings. The third component is confrontation: listening and affirming are not passive activities, and confrontation is sometimes necessary, including the questioning of socially constructed barriers to growth. Fourth is accountability to each other in the healing circle, with healing as the final step. Foster Boyd's emphasis on mutuality and communication is important for womanist pastoral theology.

Carroll Watkins Ali has developed a more extensive analysis of womanist pastoral theology in her search for a new paradigm that is more effective for African Americans. She states that in this context pastoral theology must address "the communal needs for survival and liberation [that] (1) begins with the experience of the culture versus objectifications and abstractions about the culture, (2) allows for the significance of communality versus individuality, and (3) expands the operations of ministry."[4]

Ali envisions a pastoral theology that regularly utilizes cultural sources from within the black community for ministry. These sources include African philosophical strains extant among African Americans, womanist and black liberation theologies, black literature and narrative, and black psychology.[5] Each of these cultural sources should assist ministers in adopting an "attitude of advocacy" to give birth to a ministry that is nurturing, empowering, and liberating.[6]

These are not the only expressions and analyses of pastoral theology that are developing. At Yale University, Yolanda Y. Smith has developed a "tri-collaborative model for teaching the triple-heritage." The three-level heritage includes Christian, African, and African American traditions. Each brings different sources for religious education. Smith uses the spirituals as a location where each of these heritages overlaps. Here, she contends, a model for religious education should encompass communal dialogue, creative engagement, critical reflection, and cooperative action.[7] One dynamic of her work is that she brings a full range of African American arts into her analysis as a cultural source to be mined. In this, she is like another womanist scholar, Cheryl Kirk-Duggan.

Some of Kirk-Duggan's work centered on the spirituals as a source of wisdom from and for the community. Of note here and related to Smith's work, Kirk-Duggan has crafted *African American Special Days: 15 Complete Worship Services*.[8] This text utilizes African American history, traditions, and folklore to frame ways to worship. This book, which is accessible to families, religious educators, and pastors, shapes thinking about the meaning of celebration.

Pastoral theology refers to aspects of ministering, including motivations for and processes of ministry. What doctrines and beliefs call a denomination to minister among its members or to the wider community? What is the aim of ministry? How are individuals called to ministry, and how should they be trained? These are questions of pastoral theology that are answered in different ways by different denominations.

A related but distinct field is that of ecclesiology. This field of theology studies aspects of the church itself — its structures, systems, and polity. Ecclesiology, which encompasses the formal study of the church's doctrinal development, also explores its traditions and heresies. The black denominational churches have intricate histories, each somewhat different, that have interacted with social structures and events over time. References to "the" black church are metaphorical: all African Americans do not belong to a single church. However, the metaphor refers to the social and religious realities that most African Americans have experienced. African American religious structures reflect black religious traditions, and those traditions, in turn, reflect African American experiences. One example is "jumping the broom," a form of marriage with roots in African-derived marriage ceremonies from the time of enslavement. Today, some African Americans remember this history and add a modernized form to their religious marriage ceremony.

Experiences of oppression linked with African cognitive orientations, including culture and spirituality, become the base from which womanists theologize about the meaning of church. In the past and in some cases today, church structures in black communities have generally excluded women from formal leadership roles, yet women have comprised the majority membership of black churches. Why have black women not been part of church leadership? Some theological perspectives claim that God ordained the exclusion of women from ministry. Still others argue that portions of the Pauline letters order women to be silent in church communities. These arguments have had great power in shaping the minds of church members, to the extent that women themselves will argue against other women being present in the pulpit or on the treasury board. Patricia L. Hunter, herself an ordained Baptist minister, holds that women are often the greatest blocks to inclusion of women in ministry:

> If I had a dollar for every time I heard someone say, "It is not the men in my congregation that are against women preachers, it is the women," I could begin an early retirement. Statements of how women are unsupportive of each other point to the collusion of women to undermine one another, sometimes without even knowing it.[9]

Black women, she contends, are taught to distrust and fear other women. Hunter challenges African American women to learn to love self through understanding that all people are created in God's image. To understand that all creation is created good establishes a new vision of human possibilities. This view recovers passion and power, especially for black women. She also challenges black churches to confront patriarchy and address issues of sexuality.[10]

This discussion raises the question of what is a church. A church is most often considered in terms of organized religion, such as the African Methodist Episcopal (A.M.E.) Church or the Baptist Church. A group of people identify themselves in terms of a commonly held set of beliefs and practices, including how the organization ought to operate and how the community should worship. Commitment to a particular faith confession involves the mutual development of the individual member and the believing community. The shared life of the community is of singular importance and becomes the measure for the integrity of the professed belief. In the words of the Acts of the Apostles, "The community of believers were of one heart and one mind" (Acts 4:32). The Acts of the Apostles tells stories of an early church community in which there were many disagreements. Conflict and tensions within church bodies are not new; becoming "of one heart and mind" does not happen by magic. Resolution and reconciliation must be active rather than accidental processes.

However, when women are excluded from significant leadership, the majority of membership is excluded from full participation. This critique has been made by many women and men about church structures in general, and charges of hypocrisy have driven some people away from participation in communities that lack a unified mind and heart. What then is a believer to do? Karen Baker-Fletcher sheds some insight on this dilemma. She observes that church is both transforming and transformative, operated by imperfect people and yet essential to the growth of the faith of believers. Also, church is not restricted by the day of the week or by a designated space; church happens among people. Baker-Fletcher states:

> From a womanist perspective, to speak of church as "event" or "happening" moves beyond a romanticized, religion-addicted, feel-good motivation to one that looks to the movement of Spirit in relation to *spiritual praxis*. Local churches participate in Church Universal when their members actively participate in God's aim for healing and wholeness of self, family, community, and world.[11]

This womanist concern for the wholeness of the entire community as an ecclesial focus is repeated in Emilie Townes's writings. She articulates four questions with which womanists challenge church structures: "Can we be people of faith in the midst of diversity? ... What are we teaching the people? ... What are we doing for the spiritual health of the people? ... What are we saying to the people?"[12] Townes also seeks ways to empower church members to work for social justice by ministering them into their own power.

Womanists have begun to analyze three areas that can clarify the meaning of church. These three areas are related to ecclesiology in part by definition, but also in the ways they affect churches' structures. These areas are: (1) ecumenical dialogue, (2) studies of traditional African religions, and (3) a theology of sexuality.

Ecumenical Dialogue

Womanist theologians and ethicists are not members of a single church and are located at a variety of places along a continuum from radical to conservative. However, the movement of women within their faith communities is a connection beyond denominations. Seeking the wholeness of others is bound with the intention to be true to self, and this becomes a linkage among women who are excluded within their own churches. With this connecting point, what do womanists have to contribute to a dialogue between denominations?

The black church resulted from the exclusion, oppression, and political powerlessness that stemmed from racism and that set African Americans into socially limited categories. The history of that reality is bound with the history of black people. Evelyn Brooks Higginbotham discusses the black church as a format for a black "public sphere." Since black people participated only marginally in the ruling structures of American society, the black church became a center of social life for African Americans. Churches housed insurance companies, schools, libraries, and a variety of other functions that black people could not find in other venues. Higginbotham writes: "The church also functioned as a discursive, critical arena — a public sphere in which values and issues were aired, debated, and disseminated throughout the black community."[13]

In this way, a form of ecumenism has long been operative among African American churches seeking to fight the limits of oppression. However, the methods of achieving the goal of justice have always been under debate and are sometimes discussed in terms of the differences between the ideologies of assimilation, integration, or separation. The issues at stake are more complex and never as simple as reductionist arguments claim. The same arguments are reflected in the religious realities of black people. In a ground-breaking study, Gayraud S. Wilmore, a historian, interpreted the political ideologies built into black religious thought. He asserts that by the middle of the twentieth century the black Christian church was deradicalized and black political struggles were no longer centered in the churches.[14]

Some people hold up the Civil Rights Movement as one of the symbols of cooperation among black churches. That position, however, denies the state of relations among African Americans, not all of whom were immediately appreciative of the efforts of the nonviolent activism of Martin Luther King Jr. Taylor Branch's *Parting the Waters: America in the King Years 1954–1963* demonstrates how complex and dangerous these times were.[15]

Womanists ask difficult questions about the ecumenical efforts of black churches today. Ecumenism among black churches has focused on resistance against oppression. Yet the growth of megachurches, ministers and pastors with interests beyond the communities, and church communities that seek to exclude the poor create a new reality among black people. As class differentiations among African Americans become more sharply defined, some churches seek a wealthier clientele, and "have–have not" splits are mirrored among the faithful. Delores Williams prophetically calls today's black churches to new forms of ecumenism, especially in working together for social transformation. She encourages churches to pool resources to deal with social problems in black communities; male ministers to repent of sexually and emotionally exploiting women; ministers to repent of complicity with forces that oppress black people; and churches to develop effective health and prison ministries.[16]

Another dimension of ecumenism from a womanist perspective is viewed through the eyes of Diana Hayes. As a womanist theologian who is Roman Catholic, she raises another challenge for ecumenism. Hayes has pointed out that most often black liberation and womanist theologies were believed to originate from the perspective of the denominations of which most black people are members:

> In the writings of many Black theologians, references to Black Catholics, to the Roman Catholic Church in the United States, and to the efforts toward self-expression of Black Catholics in the nineteenth and twentieth centuries, are few and far between. Black Catholics have been invisible both to those inside and outside of the Roman Catholic Church.[17]

This indicates the need for womanist theological constructions to avoid forms of religious elitism. At issue is the deconstruction of any hierarchical, elitist barriers that could be destructive of dialogue among black people or lead to the belief that there is no diversity among African Americans. Hayes's challenge extends to other religious traditions as well.

One example would be Debra Washington Mubashshir, a Muslim womanist theologian who studies the faces of African American Islam, including the roles and experiences of women. Her work will surely add to a more encompassing ecumenical dialogue.[18]

True ecumenism has the potential to shape womanist theology in the coming years. The questions of divisions among denominations and religions may surface other refinements in naming and claiming the religiosity of African American women and men, which may impact the shape of churches.

Connections with Traditional African Religions

Explorations of traditional African religions also have implications for womanist and black liberation theologies. Locating African American connections with traditional African religions is not a slip into fantasy, but a process of exploring the real shape of African American religious life today. The task takes on importance as the categories of "race" continue to shift and issues of black identities are still being discussed. Some theorists might contend that discussions of identity are passé, yet African Americans continue to seek empowering self-images amid shifting racial identities. Stuart Hall, a sociologist from England, has discussed the importance of identification and identities for political action: "Once you've got identification, you can decide which identities are working *this* week. . . . Identification means that you are called in a certain way, interpolated in a certain way. . . . That is what is at stake in this political struggle."[19]

Imagining Home: Class, Culture, and Nationalism in the African Diaspora is a volume of collected essays where each author explores some dynamics of Pan-Africanism. The editors explain that the concept of "Diaspora" entails no land and has no common language, yet many black people understand themselves as oppressed and marginalized in the Western countries of their birth, with Africa seen as an imagined home.[20] African Americans already understand the many separate identities and cultural references that mark life in the United States. This is in spite of the claim that race is peripheral to American economic and social success, that everyone has an equal opportunity to pull themselves up by their bootstraps.

In addition to political necessity, the shape of cultural identity must also be explored more fully in order to make connections to African cultural referents. Alice Eley Jones provides one example of such work in her essay "Sacred Places and Holy Ground: West African Spiritualism at Stagville Plantation." Jones writes of the structure of traditional African religions in which life was a connection between the "dead, the living and the yet unborn.... In traditional religions there were no creeds to be recited.... What Africans did was motivated by what they believed, and what they believed sprang from what they did and experienced."[21]

She demonstrates the connections between the African and the black American through her study of the material artifacts found in the cabins of enslaved Africans, such as a divining rod, a cowrie shell, or a medicine stick:

> The millions of enslaved Africans who eventually came to live in the New World were equipped to re-create the secret holy ceremonies and practices of their homeland. The old men and women moved freely among black and white plantation inhabitants. The blacks usually understood and were able to interpret the secret symbols, while for the most part they were hidden in plain view of whites.[22]

There are many links between black people in the Diaspora that still need to be discovered.[23] One method used is ethnography, which will be discussed later. Another method, like that used in the work of Alice Eley Jones, is anthropology. Zora Neale Hurston's early-twentieth-century anthropological research was unmatched for many years. Her anthropological study of the spirituality and beliefs of black people in the South of the 1920s identified structures of meaning that have yet to be fully explored.[24] Hurston listened to the folk stories of healers and conjurers, expansions on biblical figures such as Peter, and fables of symbolic characters such as High John de Conquer. In these many accounts, she found another sense of religiosity, with strong orientations in African traditional religion. Indeed, the classic collection edited by Harold

Courlander, *A Treasury of Afro-American Folklore*, includes the African Diaspora, indicating links between black people in the United States, Cuba, Haiti, Brazil, and Venezuela: "Looking at the Western Hemisphere as a whole, it is abundantly evident that many tangible elements of African ways, customs, attitudes, values and views of life survived the Atlantic crossing.... Numerous Negro communities in the Americas continue to draw from the African wellspring."[25]

Identification of the African wellspring, which was denigrated by white scholars, continues to challenge black communities. In 1991, a black community effort began to preserve the known site of the African Burial Grounds in New York City, which was about to be leveled to build a new office tower. The combined efforts of ministers, community activists, the mayor of New York City, the Congressional Black Caucus, and legislators from the State of New York worked to have the burial grounds designated as a historic landmark. Although a large portion of the burial grounds had been already destroyed, a third of the site was preserved. Anthropologists have discovered several connections between the lives of enslaved eighteenth-century black people and the continent of Africa.[26] The work in New York has expanded to other places in the country, including the Dallas Freedmen's Cemetery, spurred by great interest in the lost or hidden pieces of African American pasts.[27]

Another significant source is found in the historic narratives of black people. Carolyn Denard has reflected on the moral values of the black church located in such narratives — for example, those from W. E. B. Du Bois, Mary McLeod Bethune, and Howard Thurman. Denard states the importance of such discoveries:

> The black church tradition, as opposed to church tradition or white church tradition, was born out of an effort to interpret the ethical and moral mission of African Americans in terms that would meet the challenges they faced in this world as oppressed and disposed people — the values they used to maintain their dignity, their humanity and their faith in God.[28]

Another form of narrative is being mined by Joan M. Martin, a womanist ethicist who has utilized enslaved women's stories in order to identify their work ethic and the ordinary theologies operative in their lives. Martin expands the concept of black women's moral agency and demonstrates how it operated in the lives of enslaved women. Her aim is not to study the ideas found in these narratives as curiosities, but to draw some connections with African American women's lives today:

> Particularly in black religion, more than denomination or faith tradition, the *community* of faith is the site where individuals and social groups shape work-as-human-meaning. It is in black religious communities that meaningful human work for many black people, and especially blackwomen, is an inherited legacy, a disposition, and a practice.[29]

All of these are indications of places where the faith lives of black men and women need a conscious reconnection, in ways that are holistic and unromantic, with an African past and with the existent and overlooked African cognitive orientations. Peter J. Paris has begun this formulation with *The Spirituality of African Peoples*,[30] in which he closely observes the linkages between African American and African religious meaning systems. He broadly uses the term "syncretism" to refer to many of the ways black people created safe spaces for mental, moral, and spiritual survival/quality of life (to return to Delores Williams's term) using religious imagination.[31]

Womanists stand at the edges of this exploration of the dynamics of religious development in the African Diaspora. Emilie Townes, for example, identifies one possible direction for study: "The Christian cross introduced to slaves may have evoked a religious response that was more African in nature than Western.... The entire symbolic world of Africa did not enter directly into slave worship but the memory of those symbols was not lost completely."[32] What was the nature of the Christian religion that black people adopted? How are religious symbols to be interpreted when culture is a referent? Of particular interest to womanists is gender construction: When these African Diasporic connections are made, how are black women's gender roles constructed? These questions are being answered by research that also reaches into traditional African religious analysis. For instance, Rachel Harding's study of the historical development of African Brazilian Candomblé includes information on the roles of women in those communities.[33]

Karen Baker-Fletcher, a womanist theologian, is working with African religious themes in different ways. She notes the importance of African symbolism within the contemporary literature of black women, such as Julie Dash's film *Daughters of the Dust* and Toni Morrison's *Beloved*. "There is a scene in Dash's film in which Eli walks on water like his mythic ancestors — symbol of the power to overcome bondage and enter freedom. . . . Beloved, in Morrison's novel, moves in reverse. She walks *out* of the water, representing the *return* of historical and mythic ancestors."[34] Both Morrison and Dash emphasize the importance of water as a powerful spiritual metaphor, as well as the importance of relationships with ancestors.

Besides references to the work of others, Baker-Fletcher imbues her own work with African orientations. She notes that Christian womanists should honor the ancestors from historic African American communities who fought for black freedom and should find there the presence and spirit of Christ. She extends the concepts of ancestor and community: "Community includes the earth, which in some sense is our oldest living elder and our elemental ancestor. Jesus, who is God as dust and spirit, is organic to creation's physical and spiritual sustenance. Women as well as men are called to participate in this sustaining activity."[35] Recalled here are ideas central to African traditional religions, particularly ancestor devotion, and a cosmology that embraces all of the universe.

Carolyn McCrary has uncovered connections between African religio-philosophical concepts and Howard Thurman's concept of unity. Thurman understood person *in* community, aiming toward wholeness and transformation. The four features of Thurman's theology of community, McCrary states, are unity, actualization of potential, love, and reconciliation. Unity refers to an underlying force in the heart of all humans that aims for the fulfillment of a "corroborating unity" of all life. McCrary relates this concept of unity to the Bantu-Rwandaise philosophy of *Ntu*. "Two aspects of *Ntu* are important for us in this discussion: (1) that it is the unifying force which bespeaks the connecting essence of all that is; and

(2) that at the fundamental core, there is an interconnectedness and an interdependence of being of everyone and everything."[36]

McCrary's article is not solely about connections between African and African American concepts, but this portion of her work indicates possibilities for further studies within the academy. It is important to note that there has been a long tradition of "Africanizing" black religion, hence the *African* Methodist Episcopal (A.M.E.) Church or the African symbolism in the Masons. There are still other dynamics to consider when thinking of traditional African religion and African Americans, including membership in alternative religions.

The practice of the traditional African religion of the Yoruba has had a growing presence among African Americans. One of the most well known of its members is Iyanla Vanzant, who is a Yoruba priestess. Her numerous television appearances and books aim for wholeness of all people, with special emphasis on the needs of black women. Her book *The Value in the Valley* is subtitled *A Black Woman's Guide through Life's Dilemmas.*[37] Vanzant has constructed that book around a "Meditation with the Mother" at the beginning of each chapter, the Mother being earth/divinity/creativity. A different sense of spirituality, one that resonates well with African American women, is presented throughout the book and is not affiliated with organized Christian religion.

Explorations of the connections of African Americans with traditional African religions have already impacted the black churches. Church communities have found ways to incorporate African-oriented rites, such as the development of rites of passage for young women and men. Those programs connect the young of the congregation with the elders, encourage intergenerational dialogue, and build individual self-esteem and community bonds. Many church communities also sponsor trips to various African countries. The church communities that have most thoroughly steeped themselves in the African and black American connection have been the Shrines of the Black Madonna. With communities in Detroit, Houston, and Atlanta, the members identify themselves as the Pan-African Orthodox Church and work to incorporate the cultural perspectives of the black Diaspora.

African American churches will continue to be shaped by theology that incorporates African cultural dynamics, while raising up components of traditional African religion within their own cultural perspectives.

Theology of Sexuality

As they revisit constructions of gender, womanists have challenged the black community at all levels to take a serious look at the ways sexuality has been used to cripple the members. Toinette Eugene, a womanist ethicist, has taken leadership on these issues. She often addresses issues of domestic violence in African American communities, for domestic and sexual violence are symptomatic of distorted sexuality in black communities.[38] Eugene writes of the connections between spirituality and sexuality in black communities and the lack of response on the part of black churches: "One of the most neglected ministries in the black church has been the holistic integration of sexuality and life."[39] If Christian spirituality infuses all of life, then black sexuality is not exempt. Eugene charges that "a black liberating love must serve as the linchpin to link black spirituality and sexuality."[40]

Kelly Brown Douglas has developed the fullest statement of a womanist theology of sexuality by drawing on the work of Alice Walker, Toinette Eugene, bell hooks, Cheryl Townsend Gilkes, Angela Davis, and others. Womanist theologians, Douglas asserts, are particularly compelled to address black sexuality. She cites Alice Walker's definition of "womanist," which calls for wholeness of all people and a belief in a God of justice: "Womanist theology affirms those understandings of God, Christ, and other aspects of Black faith that promote the life and wholeness of all Black folks while disavowing those that do not."[41] The aim of a womanist theology of sexuality is to heal the "life-defying brokenness in the Black community" that results from the current construction of black sexuality as a pawn of white culture:

> The community is ravaged by teenage pregnancies, homicide, HIV/AIDS, domestic violence, and even sexual misconduct among clergy and other Black leaders. Moreover the Black

church...has been shamefully unresponsive to these issues even while it provides a sacred canopy for sexist and hetero-sexist structures and behavior.[42]

Douglas calls for a sexual discourse of resistance that takes into account the idea that all humans are created in God's image, that embodies Jesus' incarnation as transformative possibility, and that understands that God's passion is "divine energy within human beings, the love of God, that compels them toward life-giving, life-producing, and life-affirming activity and relationships."[43] This discourse can initiate new conversations among African Americans about heterosexual and homosexual relationships and their meaning to the community.

Douglas's statement of a womanist theology of sexuality has particular implications for African American women. Gender entrapment continues to mar black women's relationships as they struggle against stereotypes. Amoral Jezebel, safe Mammy, and castrating Sapphire are stereotypes that construct some negative form of black women's sexuality. A Christian womanist sexual discourse of resistance, based on human- and God-created goodness, will destroy the power that Mammy, Sapphire, and Jezebel have over black women's self-image and esteem. Such a discourse will change communal perceptions of black women, of men, and of sexual preference. The fearful images that demand that black families look exactly like white nuclear families will also lose their power of social condemnation, which in the past has been useful to force compliance. Douglas has sent out a call for a nonviolent resistance movement to seek human rights.

A Christian womanist sexual discourse of resistance has potential to alter churches in black communities, particularly if restrictions against women in ministry or the pulpit are lifted. Spiritual gifts will be judged without consideration of gender. Ministries to prevent and heal all forms of domestic violence, social violence, illness, and oppression will be welcomed. Churches will no longer serve as breeding grounds for sexism, but will offer safe space — sanctuary — for all.

Certainly there are already churches in black communities that work in this healing way. Delores Williams refers to churches that work for liberation and "survival and positive quality of life formation for all black people. This is when the black church emerges from the soul of communal memory. For the black church — having neither denominational commitment nor religious bias — acts as the great judging, healing, fighting, holy Godforce."[44]

This vision of church encompasses many of the womanist pastoral and ecclesial objectives. The vision is neither simple to construct nor easy to achieve. Womanist views of pastoral theology and ecclesiology demonstrate several components of womanist theology: the importance of linking theory with the practices of social activism, the need to create safe spaces, a return to Alice Walker's definition of womanist in evaluating theological constructions, use of critical social analysis, and support for dialogue and openness. Womanist theology will make use of new methodologies to expand these ideas into other areas of theology.

Ethnography and Art: Expanding Womanist Methods

Ethnography has the potential to become a powerful tool for defining black women's life experiences, while art shows truths that are beyond words. Womanists are increasingly realizing that ethnography and art can make significant contributions in the same ways that history and sociology have.

Ethnography is closely related to cultural anthropology and their research methods are similar. Zora Neale Hurston studied anthropology with Franz Boas in the 1920s, and her pioneering work, *The Sanctified Church*,[45] provides an important study of black religious folk meaning in the South. Ruth Landes, the daughter of Russian Jewish immigrants, became interested in African American culture around the same time period as Hurston and later became a student of Boas. Her classic 1947 study of Candomblé religious society in Brazil, *The City of Women*,[46] brought to light a religion in which black women held key roles, in which race and gender were structured differently, and whose African roots were obvious. These studies were not well received by most anthropologists of the day because the subjects were considered too exotic and the studies not sufficiently scholarly.

Since the 1960s, anthropologists and ethnographers have shifted position, understanding that there are different ways of analyzing culture. Renato Rosaldo, an anthropologist, has explored the importance of the participant observer:

> The social analyst's multiple identities at once underscore the potential for uniting an analytical with an ethical project and render obsolete the view of the utterly detached observer who looks down from on high. Rather than work downward from abstract principles, social critics work outward from in depth knowledge of a specific form of life. Informed by such conceptions as social justice, human dignity and equality, they use their moral imagination to move from the world as it actually is to a locally persuasive vision of how it should be.[47]

African Americans who do research on black people are seldom considered impartial objective researchers. Womanists, in turn, are intentionally passionate about centering black women's realities.

Linda E. Thomas, a womanist theologian, has developed connections between ethnography and womanist methodology in her research. She urges womanist scholars to further the development of theology by adopting the tools of ethnography: "Not only should womanist scholars include historical texts and literature in our theological constructs and reconstruction of knowledge, but we should also embrace a research process which engages poor black women who are living human documents."[48] Thomas envisions a "womanist anthropology of survival and liberation" that guards against claims of objectivity and the tendency toward distance that occurs in some research methods:

> Ideally, the womanist scholar is an indigenous anthropologist — that is, one who reflects critically upon her own community of origin and brings a sensitivity to the political, economic, and cultural systems which impact poor and working class black women being studied. At the same time she gives priority to the life story of the subject in a way that

underscores the narratives of a long line of subjugated voices from the past to the present.[49]

Thomas contends that this method will aid the reconstruction of knowledge, the epistemological framework within which each person operates.

Sociologist Cheryl Townsend Gilkes presents another vision of ethnography in her reading of literature, specifically Alice Walker's *The Color Purple*. Gilkes's use of literature as womanist analysis straddles ethnography and art. Gilkes recognizes that *The Color Purple* is not technically an ethnographic study, that the novel inscribes black women's lives into sharp relief through a

> prophetic critique of oppression and its consequences.... [T]he complexities of social class are a critical focus.... Walker highlights the importance of the discovery of agency, resources, and social position through a variety of experiences in the life of one Black woman, poor by her own definition.[50]

Gilkes is not urging scholars to use literature *instead* of the real lives of black women, but is calling for the use of every resource at hand to analyze the sophisticated structures of daily reality in order to better understand and state these complexities. In Gilkes's analysis, the reading of *The Color Purple* is, in Thomas's term, ethno-history.

The arts and performance are also terrain rich with possibilities for womanist scholars to unveil formerly invisible dimensions of black women's lives. Jualynne Dodson at the University of Colorado has long been involved in uncovering Diasporic connections in her work with the Festival del Caribe.[51] This week-long conference researches a variety of African-Atlantic connections, including music and dance. Both Yolanda Smith's work in the use of spirituals for religious education and Cheryl Kirk-Duggan's use of spirituals and blues as texts to understand black women follow this approach.

As an example of a project in development, Jeannette Murrell and her daughter, Jasmine, are completing a video in Detroit titled *Unheard Voices,* featuring the "unheard" voices of black women.

Jeannette Murrell's mother, Margaret E. Allen, has long been a community activist in New York City. Allen calls herself a feminist and has been involved with a variety of movements in her eighty-plus years of life. Allen's sister, Jean Capers, will also be interviewed. Capers was the first African American woman to serve on the city council in Cleveland. Jasmine Murrell will assist in taping the grandmother and aunt.

Such projects are about the power of self-definition, making use of tools in ways that redefine knowledge itself. In the words of Linda Thomas:

> Admittedly, reconstructing knowledge is like tearing down a formidable edifice that has been built over an extensive number of years.... A womanist, in her reconstruction of knowledge, must not only be a diligent craft person, she must develop an approach that utilizes the kind of technology that can dismantle the seeming indestructibility of the original building materials.[52]

Conclusion

Theology is a creative human enterprise that reflects the social and political realities of human groups. As such, each theology develops over time, adjusting as human social and political realities change. Theology as a reflection of humanity demonstrates the diversity of ways that people — wherever they may be — encounter and name the Divine. One danger all people face is their illogical assumption that the way they view God is the only correct way. The rise in diverse theological voices, particularly at the end of the twentieth century, has contributed to the deconstruction of the notion that there is only one valid theological perspective.

Womanists generally view theology as "God-talk," a way of thinking that keeps the human dimension front and center. For womanists, God-talk must encompass both words and actions in divine-to-human and human-to-human contacts. This contrasts with the idea that theology can be a "study of God," a process that abstracts theology and blurs the lines of the human activity.

Womanist theology is a continuing project that participates in the ongoing, fully human effort to refine God-talk.

Discussion Questions

1. In your faith community, can you identify traditions that have roots in a given culture? Can you identify other cultural dynamics that operate in this or another religious community?

2. Do you think faith communities should be involved in social activism? Why or why not?

3. Define and state the purposes of a Christian womanist sexual discourse of resistance.

4. Is there an elderly black woman in your life or community who was a "womanist" before the term was coined? Consider your earlier definition of womanist theology in your answer.

5. Look for artistic renderings of black women. These can be paintings or sculpture. Are there any themes that surface in these works? Are there any differences when the artist is a black woman?

Notes

Chapter 1: Black Women: Race, Gender, and Class

1. Cheryl Townsend Gilkes, " 'Some Mother's Son and Some Father's Daughter': Gender and Biblical Language in Afro-Christian Worship Tradition," in *Shaping New Visions: Gender and Values in American Culture*, ed. Clarissa W. Atkinson, Constance Hall Buchanan, and Margaret R. Miles (Ann Arbor, Mich.: UMI Research Press, 1987), 80–81.

2. Delores Williams, "The Color of Feminism: Or Speaking the Black Woman's Tongue," *Journal of Religious Thought* 43 (1986): 52.

3. Katie G. Cannon, *Black Womanist Ethics* (Atlanta: Scholars Press, 1988).

4. Jacquelyn Grant, *White Women's Christ, Black Women's Jesus: Feminist Christology and Womanist Response* (Atlanta: Scholars Press, 1989).

5. Renita Weems, *Just a Sister Away: A Womanist Vision of Women's Relationships in the Bible* (San Diego: LuraMedia Press, 1988).

6. Carla F. Peterson, *"Doers of the Word": African American Women Speakers and Writers in the North, 1830–1880* (New York: Oxford University Press, 1995), 7.

7. Beth Richie, *Compelled to Crime: The Gender Entrapment of Battered Black Women* (New York: Routledge, 1996).

8. bell hooks, *Sisters of the Yam: Black Women, and Self-Recovery* (Boston: South End Press, 1993).

9. Ibid., 89.

10. Ibid., 190.

11. Ibid., 129.

12. Stephanie Y. Mitchem, *Getting Off the Cross: African American Women, Health, and Salvation* (Ann Arbor, Mich.: UMI Dissertation Services, 1998), 105.

13. Linda Kalof and Bruce Wade, "Sexual Attitudes and Experiences with Sexual Coercion: Exploring the Influence of Race and Gender," *Journal of Black Psychology* 21, no. 3 (August 1995): 237–38.

14. Patricia J. Williams, *The Alchemy of Race and Rights: Diary of a Law Professor* (Cambridge, Mass.: Harvard University Press, 1991), 119–20.

15. Evelyn Brooks Higginbotham, "African American Women's History and the Metalanguage of Race," in *We Specialize in the Wholly Impossible": A Reader in Black Women's History,* ed. Darlene Clark Hine, Wilma King, and Linda Reed (Brooklyn, N.Y.: Carlson Publishing, 1995), 5.

16. Peterson, *"Doers of the Word,"* 20.

17. Dorothy Roberts, "The Value of Black Mothers' Work," *Radical America* 26, no. 1 (1996): 12.

18. Cheryl Townsend Gilkes, "The Loves and Troubles of African-American Women's Bodies: The Womanist Challenge to Cultural Humiliation and Community Ambivalence," in *Troubling in My Soul: Womanist Perspectives on Evil and Suffering,* ed. Emilie M. Townes (Maryknoll, N.Y.: Orbis Books, 1993), 239–40.

19. Susan Willis, *Specifying: Black Women Writing the American Experience* (Madison: University of Wisconsin Press, 1987), 6.

20. Kathleen Thompson and Hilary MacAustin, eds., *The Face of Our Past: Images of Black Women from Colonial America to the Present* (Bloomington: Indiana University Press, 1999).

21. Kibibi V. C. Mack, *Parlor Ladies and Ebony Drudges: African American Women, Class, and Work in a South Carolina Community* (Nashville: University of Tennessee Press, 1999).

22. Emily Hoffnar and Michael Greene, "Residential Location and the Earnings of African American Women," in *African Americans and Post-industrial Labor Markets,* ed. J. B. Stewart (New Brunswick, N.J.: Transaction Publishers, 1997), 244. The study focuses on the impact an urban or suburban location may have on the earnings potential of black women.

23. Carolyn Ratcliff, unpublished paper, June 2000.

24. Rogers M. Smith, "Toward a More Perfect Union: Beyond Old Liberalism and Neoliberalism," in *Without Justice for All,* ed. Adolph Reed Jr. (Boulder, Colo.: Westview Press, 1999), 328.

25. Andrew Hacker, *Two Nations: Black and White, Separate, Hostile, Unequal* (New York: Charles Scribner's Sons, 1992).

26. Ibid., 231.

27. Adolph Reed Jr., *Class Notes: Posing as Politics and Other Thoughts on the American Scene* (New York: The New Press, 2000), 98.

28. Leith Mullings, *On Our Own Terms: Race, Class, and Gender in the Lives of African American Women* (New York: Routledge, 1997), 48.

29. bell hooks, *Where We Stand: Class Matters* (New York: Routledge, 2000), 17.

30. Ibid., 61.

31. Patricia Hill Collins, *Fighting Words: Black Women and the Search for Justice* (Minneapolis: University of Minnesota Press, 1998), 36, 38.

32. Michele Wallace, "Variations on Negation and the Heresy of Black Feminist Creativity," in *Reading Black, Reading Feminist: A Critical Anthology,* ed. Henry Louis Gates Jr. (New York: Meridian Books, 1990), 55.

33. Patricia Hill Collins, *Black Feminist Thought: Knowledge, Consciousness, and the Politics of Empowerment,* vol. 2, *Perspectives on Gender* (New York: Routledge, 1990), 165.

34. Mullings, *On Our Own Terms,* 6.

35. Janice N. Tillman, unpublished paper, June 2000.

36. Wallace, "Variations on Negations," 66.

37. bell hooks, *Teaching to Transgress: Education as the Practice of Freedom* (New York: Routledge, 1994), 67.

38. Delores S. Williams, *Sisters in the Wilderness: The Challenge of Womanist God-Talk* (Maryknoll, N.Y.: Orbis Books, 1993), 246.

39. JoAnne Marie Terrell, *Power in the Blood: The Cross in the African American Experience* (Maryknoll, N.Y.: Orbis Books, 1998), 188.

Chapter 2: Constructing Theologies

1. There have been a variety of scholars involved in these analytical processes, from a variety of countries. A small sampling includes the following: Michel Foucault (philosophy), *Discipline and Punish: The Birth of the Prison* (New York: Schocken, 1979), deconstructs modern concepts of punishment; Cheikh Anta Diop (history), *The African Origin of Civilization: Myth or Reality* (Westport, Conn.: Lawrence Hill, 1974), deconstructs histories that privilege Greco-Roman and European perspectives; Edward Said (social criticism), *Orientalism* (Harmondsworth, England: Penguin, 1978), critiques the social construction of groups called "Orientals"; Michelle Zimbalist Rosaldo and Louise Lamphere, eds. (anthropology), *Woman, Culture, and Society* (Stanford, Calif.: Stanford University Press, 1974), offer the works of several authors who take apart the social construction of gender.

2. See Virginia Fabella, M.M., and R. S. Sugirtharajah, eds., *Dictionary of Third World Theologies* (Maryknoll, N.Y.: Orbis Books, 2000), which distinguishes between differing perspectives. Note definitions of "Liberation" (122–24), "Liberation Theologies" (127–29), and "Third World Theologies in the First World" (204–17).

3. Robert E. Hood, *Begrimed and Black: Christian Traditions on Blacks and Blackness* (Minneapolis: Fortress Press, 1994).

4. Ibid., 139.

5. David Walker, *An Appeal to the Coloured Citizens of the World* (New York: Hill and Wang, 1965), 7.

6. Ibid., 42.

7. Michele Wallace, *Black Macho and the Myth of Superwoman* (reprint; New York: Warner Books, 1980).

8. Ibid., 129.

9. The Moynihan Report (1965) was officially titled *The Negro Family: The Case for National Action.* Stephen Steinberg, a sociologist, identifies this report as pivotal in the shift away from civil rights activism in the United States. Steinberg cites the report: "At the center of the tangle of pathology is the weakness of [black] family structure. Once or twice removed, it will be found to be the principal source of most of the aberrant, inadequate, or antisocial behavior that did not establish, but now serves to perpetuate, the cycle of poverty and deprivation" (Stephen Steinberg, "The Liberal Retreat from Race during the Post–Civil Rights Era," in *The House That Race Built: Black Americans, U.S. Terrain*, ed. Wahneema Lubiano [New York: Pantheon Books, 1997], 26). Hence, instead of being racism's effects, the black victims are blamed for their social ills.

10. Kenneth Stampp, *The Peculiar Institution: Slavery in the Antebellum South* (New York: Vintage Books, 1955), 158.

11. Mary Romero and Debbie Storrs, " 'Is That Sociology?' The Accounts of Women of Color Graduate Students in Ph.D. Programs," in *Women Leading in Education*, ed. Diane M. Dunlap and Patricia A. Schmuck (Albany: State University of New York Press, 1995), 75.

12. Stuart Hall, "Subjects in History: Making Diasporic Identities," in *The House That Race Built*, 296.

13. Cornel West, afterword to *The House That Race Built*, 301–2.

14. John S. Mbiti, *African Religions and Philosophy* (New York: Anchor Books, 1970).

15. Hood, *Begrimed*, 182.

16. Emilie M. Townes, *In a Blaze of Glory: Womanist Spirituality as Social Witness* (Nashville: Abingdon Press, 1995), 77.

17. Hood, *Begrimed*, 183.

18. Luis Pedraja, *Jesus Is My Uncle: Christology from a Hispanic Perspective* (Nashville: Abingdon Press, 1999), 31.

19. Ibid., 25.

20. Ivone Gebara, "Women Doing Theology in Latin America," in *Feminist Theology from the Third World*, ed. Ursula King (Maryknoll, N.Y.: Orbis Books, 1994), 49.

21. Chung Hyun Kyung, *Struggle to Be the Sun Again: Introducing Asian Women's Theology* (Maryknoll, N.Y.: Orbis Books, 1990), 100–101.

22. Noel L. Erskine, *Decolonizing Theology: A Caribbean Perspective* (Maryknoll, N.Y.: Orbis Books, 1981), 9.

23. James H. Cone, *Black Theology and Black Power* (New York: Seabury Press, 1969).

24. Josiah Young, *A Pan-African Theology* (Trenton, N.J.: Africa World Press, 1992).

25. Ibid., 10–11.

26. Garth Kasimu Baker-Fletcher, *Xodus: An African American Male Journey* (Minneapolis: Fortress Press, 1996).

27. James H. Cone, *Risks of Faith: The Emergence of a Black Theology of Liberation, 1968–1998* (Boston: Beacon Press, 1999), 134.

28. Sidney W. Mintz and Richard Price, *The Birth of African American Culture: An Anthropological Perspective* (Boston: Beacon Press, 1976 [preface 1992]).

29. Albert Raboteau, "The Afro-American Traditions," in *Caring and Curing: Health and Medicine in the Western Religious Traditions*, ed. Ronald L. Numbers and Darrel W. Amundsen (New York: Macmillan Publishing Co., 1986), 542.

30. Lawrence W. Levine, *Black Culture and Black Consciousness: Afro-American Folk Thought from Slavery to Freedom* (New York: Oxford University Press, 1977), 63.

31. Marcia Riggs, *Can I Get a Witness? Prophetic Religious Voices of African American Women* (Maryknoll, N.Y.: Orbis Books, 1997), xi.

Chapter 3: Womanist Theology

1. Stephanie Y. Mitchem, *Getting Off the Cross: African American Women, Health, and Salvation* (Ann Arbor, Mich.: UMI Dissertation Services, 1998), 113.

2. Philomena Essed, *Understanding Everyday Racism: An Interdisciplinary Theory* (Newbury Park, Calif.: Sage Publications, 1991).

3. Darlene Clark Hine, *Hine Sight: Black Women and the Reconstruction of American History* (Brooklyn, N.Y.: Carlson Publishing, 1994), xxii.

4. Cited in Paula Giddings, *When and Where I Enter: The Impact of Black Women on Race and Sex in America* (New York: Bantam Books, 1984), 100.

5. For more information on the black women's club movement, see Gerda Lerner, ed., *Black Women in White America: A Documentary History* (New York: Vintage Books, 1973), 433–520, which excerpts primary documents from the movement. See also Giddings, *When and Where I Enter* (108–17), for an interpretation of the significance of the black women's club movement.

6. Evelyn Brooks Higginbotham, *Righteous Discontent: The Women's Movement in the Black Baptist Church, 1880–1920* (Cambridge, Mass.: Harvard University Press, 1993).

7. Patricia Hill Collins, *Black Feminist Thought: Knowledge, Consciousness, and the Politics of Empowerment* (New York: Routledge, 1990), 118.

8. Ibid.

9. Carol Boyce Davies, "Mothering and Healing in Recent Black Women's Fiction," *Sage* 2, no. 1 (spring 1985): 41.

10. Ibid., 43.

11. Toinette M. Eugene, "Regardless: An Attitude of Being for Women under Fire," *Update: Newsletter of the Evangelical and Ecumenical Women's Caucus,* 14, no. 3 (winter 1990/91): 23–34.

12. Ibid., 4.

13. Mitchem, *Getting Off the Cross,* 89.

14. Ibid., 90.

15. This construct names the multiple denominations of black religious life. These multiple churches sometimes collaborate and sometimes compete. However, common historical and sociocultural threads make strong connections. For example, see Gayraud S. Wilmore, *Black Religion and Black Radicalism: An Interpretation of the Religious History of Afro-American People,* 2d ed. (Maryknoll, N.Y.: Orbis Books, 1998); Albert J. Raboteau, *Canaan Land: A Religious History of African Americans* (New York: Oxford University Press, 2001).

16. A classic study of black religious life across the African Diaspora is George Eaton Simpson, *Black Religion in the New World* (New York: Columbia University Press, 1978).

17. In Walter E. Fluker and Catherine Tumber, eds., *A Strange Freedom: The Best of Howard Thurman on Religious Experience and Public Life* (Boston: Beacon Press, 1998), 71.

18. Cheryl Townsend Gilkes, *If It Wasn't for the Women* (Maryknoll, N.Y.: Orbis Books, 2000).

19. Black men sometimes considered Martha Jean a nuisance, believing her advice created adversarial relationships in their homes. For instance, the Queen would announce on her radio program when the factory workers at Ford Motor Company or General Motors, mostly men, would receive their annual profit-sharing checks, and the expected amounts, information some men shared in an arbitrary fashion with their wives.

20. Alice Walker, *In Search of Our Mothers' Gardens* (San Diego: Harcourt Brace Jovanovich, 1983), xi–xii.

21. Ibid.

22. Barbara Hilkert Andolsen, *Daughters of Jefferson, Daughters of Bootblacks: Racism and American Feminism* (Macon, Ga.: Mercer University Press, 1986).

23. Toinette M. Eugene, "Moral Values and Black Womanists," *Journal of Religious Thought,* 44 (winter–spring 1988): 26.

24. Katie G. Cannon, *Katie's Canon: Womanism and the Soul of the Black Community* (New York: Continuum, 1995), 23.

25. Mitchem, *Getting Off the Cross*, 18.

26. Ibid., 105.

27. Dorothy L. Pennington, *African American Women Quitting the Workplace* (Lewiston, N.Y.: Edwin Mellen Press, 1999).

28. Cannon, *Katie's Canon*, 24.

29. In Belinda Hurmence, ed., *My Folks Don't Want Me to Talk about Slavery: Twenty-One Oral Histories of Former North Carolina Slaves* (Winston-Salem, N.C.: John F. Blair, 1984), 1–2.

30. Delores Williams, *Sisters in the Wilderness: The Challenge of Womanist God-Talk* (Maryknoll, N.Y.: Orbis Books, 1993), xiv.

31. Cannon, *Katie's Canon*, 24.

32. Williams, *Sisters*, 216.

33. Ibid., 216–17; emphasis added.

34. Cannon, *Katie's Canon*, 136–37.

Chapter 4: Womanist Constructions

1. Katie G. Cannon, *Black Womanist Ethics* (Atlanta: Scholars Press, 1988), 1.

2. Ibid., 68.

3. Renita Weems, *Just a Sister Away: A Womanist Vision of Women's Relationships in the Bible* (San Diego: LuraMedia Press, 1988), ix.

4. Ibid., 1. Delores Williams significantly expanded the exploration of Hagar's role in the spiritual understandings of black women, a subject that will be discussed later in this chapter.

5. Jacquelyn Grant, *White Women's Christ, Black Women's Jesus: Feminist Christology and Womanist Response* (Atlanta: Scholars Press, 1989), 200.

6. Ibid., 209.

7. Ibid., 219, 221.

8. This black feminist/womanist dialogue will be discussed in chapter 5 below.

9. Darlene Clark Hine, *Black Women in American History*, vols. 1–16 (Brooklyn, N.Y.: Carlson Publishing, 1990).

10. Hine has written her own reflection on her work in *Hine Sight: Black Women and the Re-construction of American History* (Brooklyn, N.Y.: Carlson Publishing, 1994).

11. See also Darlene Clark Hine, Wilma King, and Linda Reed, eds., *"We Specialize in the Wholly Impossible": A Reader in Black Women's History* (Brooklyn, N.Y.: Carlson Publishing, 1995).

12. Patricia Hill Collins, *Fighting Words: Black Women and the Search for Justice* (Minneapolis: University of Minnesota Press, 1998), 198–99.

13. Emilie M. Townes, *Womanist Justice, Womanist Hope* (Atlanta: Scholars Press, 1993).

14. Emilie M. Townes, ed., *A Troubling in My Soul: Womanist Perspectives on Evil and Suffering* (Maryknoll, N.Y.: Orbis Books, 1994).

15. Marcia Riggs, *Awake, Arise, and Act: A Womanist Call for Black Liberation* (Cleveland: Pilgrim Press, 1994).

16. She notes these three in her final chapter, "Socioreligious Moral Vision for the Twenty-First Century," stating, "These elements, deriving from the club women's moral vision of God's justice and justice for the black community as a command of God, are critical for rethinking our ethical responses to interactive processes of oppression . . . and for formulating a moral vision" (ibid., 93–98).

17. Emilie M. Townes, *In a Blaze of Glory: Womanist Spirituality as Social Witness* (Nashville: Abingdon Press, 1995).

18. Ibid., 11.

19. Katie G. Cannon, *Katie's Canon: Womanism and the Soul of the Black Community* (New York: Continuum, 1995).

20. Ibid., 136–41.

21. Joan M. Martin, *More Than Chains or Toil: A Christian Work Ethic of Enslaved Women* (Louisville: Westminster John Knox Press, 2000).

22. Ibid., 11.

23. Ibid., 28, 29.

24. Townes, *In a Blaze of Glory*, 121, 123.

25. Delores Williams, *Sisters in the Wilderness: The Challenge of Womanist God-Talk* (Maryknoll, N.Y.: Orbis Books, 1993), xiv.

26. Ibid., 5–6.

27. Ibid., 216.

28. Ibid., 12.

29. Ibid.

30. In Virginia Fabella, M.M., and R. S. Sugirtharajah, eds., *Dictionary of Third World Theologies* (Maryknoll, N.Y.: Orbis Books, 2000), 222.

Chapter 5: Dialogue and Womanist Theology

1. Delores Williams, "Womanist Theology: Black Women's Voices," in *Weaving the Visions: New Patterns in Feminist Spirituality*, ed. Judith Plaskow and Carol P. Christ (San Francisco: Harper Collins, 1989), 183. In addition to dialogue, Williams lists several other aims of womanist theology: the liturgical (found in celebration of life); the confessional (found in self-love and personal integrity); the ecumenical (found in being respon-

sible for spiritual development across the lines of organized religion); and the pedagogical (found in teaching, witnessing, and sharing the wisdom of womanist ideas).

2. Sheron C. Patterson, *New Faith: A Black Christian Woman's Guide to Reformation, Re-creation, Rediscovery, Renaissance, Resurrection, and Revival* (Minneapolis: Fortress Press, 2000), 27, 28.

3. Delores Williams, *Sisters in the Wilderness: The Challenge of Womanist God-Talk* (Maryknoll, N.Y.: Orbis Books, 1993), 161.

4. Patricia A. Schechter, "'All the Intensity of My Nature': Ida B. Wells, Anger, and Politics," *Radical History Review* 70 (winter 1998): 56.

5. Patricia Hill Collins, *Fighting Words: Black Women and the Search for Justice* (Minneapolis: University of Minnesota Press, 1998), 62.

6. Ibid., 64.

7. Joy James, *Shadowboxing: Representations of Black Feminist Politics* (New York: St. Martin's Press, 1999), 11–12.

8. Ibid., 10.

9. Katie G. Cannon, *Katie's Canon: Womanism and the Soul of the Black Community* (New York: Continuum, 1995), 131.

10. Elisabeth Schüssler Fiorenza, "Transforming the Legacy of *The Woman's Bible*," in *Searching the Scriptures: A Feminist Introduction,* vol. 1, ed. Elisabeth Schüssler Fiorenza (New York: Crossroad, 1993), 15.

11. Cannon, *Katie's Canon*, 130.

12. Bonnie J. Miller-McLemore and B. Gill-Austern, eds., *Feminist and Womanist Pastoral Theology* (Nashville: Abingdon Press, 1999), 10.

13. A few examples of such comparative studies are Joy James, *Transcending the Talented Tenth: Black Leaders and American Intellectuals* (New York: Routledge, 1997); Paul Gilroy, *The Black Atlantic: Modernity and Double Consciousness* (Cambridge, Mass.: Harvard University Press, 1993); Sterling Stuckey, *Slave Culture: Nationalist Theory and the Foundations of Black America* (New York: Oxford University Press, 1987); and Hazel V. Carby, *Reconstructing Womanhood: The Emergence of the Afro-American Woman Novelist* (New York: Oxford University Press, 1987).

14. Maulana Karenga, *Introduction to Black Studies*, 3d ed. (Los Angeles: University of Sankore Press, 2002), 47.

15. Lorine Cummings, "A Womanist Response to the Afrocentric Idea: Jarena Lee, Womanist Preacher," in *Living the Intersection: Womanism and Afrocentrism in Theology,* ed. Cheryl Sanders (Minneapolis: Fortress Press, 1995), 57.

16. Yvonne R. Bell, Cathy L. Bouie, and Joseph Baldwin, "Afrocentric Cultural Consciousness and African American Male-Female Relationships," in *Afrocentric Visions: Studies in Culture and Communication,*

ed. Janice D. Hamlet (Thousand Oaks, Calif.: Sage Publications, 1998),
47–72.

17. Ibid., 64.

18. One study that explored this dilemma was Victor Anderson, *Beyond Ontological Blackness: An Essay on African American Religious and Cultural Criticism* (New York: Continuum, 1995). Anderson raised uncomfortable questions about the meaning of "blackness," its role in creating religious and cultural meaning, and the distortions that result from making racial identity a focal point.

19. Delores S. Williams, "Afrocentrism and Male-Female Relationships in Church and Society," in *Living the Intersection,* 50.

20. Ibid., 53.

21. Kanishka Chowdhury, "Afrocentric Voices: Constructing Identities, (Dis)Placing Difference," in *Race-ing Representation: Voice, History, and Sexuality,* ed. K. Myrsiades and L. Myrsiades (Lanham, Md.: Rowan and Littlefield Publishers, 1998), 28.

22. Karenga, *Introduction to Black Studies,* 335.

23. Ibid., 329.

24. Ibid., 330–31.

25. Williams, *Sisters in the Wilderness,* 169–70.

26. James Cone, "Looking Back, Going Forward: Black Theology as Public Theology," in *Black Faith and Public Talk: Critical Essays on James H. Cone's "Black Theology and Black Power,"* ed. Dwight N. Hopkins (Maryknoll, N.Y.: Orbis Books, 1999), 255.

27. James H. Cone, *Risks of Faith: The Emergence of a Black Theology of Liberation, 1968–1998* (Boston: Beacon Press, 1999), 134.

28. Dwight N. Hopkins, *Introducing Black Theology of Liberation* (Maryknoll, N.Y.: Orbis Books, 1999), 125.

29. James Ella James, "It's How the *Women* 'Read' Their 'Titles Clear,'" in *African Americans and the Bible: Sacred Texts and Social Textures,* ed. Vincent L. Wimbush (New York: Continuum, 2001), 841.

30. Valerie E. James, unpublished paper, November 2001.

31. Patterson, *New Faith,* 138.

32. Williams, *Sisters in the Wilderness,* 208–9.

33. Cannon, *Katie's Canon,* 136–37.

34. Cheryl Townsend Gilkes, *If It Wasn't for the Women* (Maryknoll, N.Y.: Orbis Books, 2001), 4, 7.

35. Kelly Brown Douglas, "Teaching Womanist Theology," in *Living the Intersection,* 153.

36. Ibid., 155.

37. Cannon, *Katie's Canon,* 137.

38. Patterson, *New Faith,* 13.

39. Countries are designated "third world" because they are considered to be in a nationwide economic development process, moving toward industrialization.

40. Ursula King, ed., *Feminist Theology from the Third World: A Reader* (Maryknoll, N.Y.: Orbis Books, 1995), 11.

41. Bette Ekeya, "Woman, for How Long Not?" in *Feminist Theology from the Third World*, 139.

42. Grace Eneme, "Women as Living Stones," in *Feminist Theology from the Third World*, 216.

43. Mercy Amba Oduyoye and Roina Fa'atauva'a, "The Struggle about Women's Theological Education," in *Feminist Theology from the Third World*, 171.

44. Virginia Fabella, M.M., and R. S. Sugirtharajah, eds., *Dictionary of Third World Theologies* (Maryknoll, N.Y.: Orbis Books, 2000), 218.

Chapter 6: Womanist Theology, Constructed

1. Jacquelyn Grant, *White Women's Christ, Black Women's Jesus: Feminist Christology and Womanist Response* (Atlanta: Scholars Press, 1989), 219, 221.

2. Jacquelyn Grant, "Womanist Jesus and the Mutual Struggle for Liberation," in *The Recovery of Black Presence*, ed. Randall C. Bailey and Jacquelyn Grant (Nashville: Abingdon Press, 1995), 130. The Ntozake Shange reference is from *For Colored Girls Who Have Considered Suicide When the Rainbow is Enuf* (New York: Macmillan, 1977), 43.

3. Jacquelyn Grant, "Womanist Theology: Black Women's Experience as a Source for Doing Theology, with Special Reference to Christology," in *African American Religious Studies: An Interdisciplinary Anthology*, ed. Gayraud Wilmore (Durham, N.C.: Duke University Press, 1989), 219.

4. M. Shawn Copeland, "Wading through Many Sorrows: Toward a Theology of Suffering in Womanist Perspective," in *A Troubling in My Soul: Womanist Perspectives on Evil and Suffering*, ed. Emilie M. Townes (Maryknoll, N.Y.: Orbis Books, 1993), 109.

5. Ibid., 118–22.

6. Ibid., 124.

7. Cheryl Kirk-Duggan, "Justified, Sanctified, and Redeemed: Blessed Expectation in Black Women's Blues and Gospels," in *Embracing the Spirit: Womanist Perspectives on Hope, Salvation, and Transformation*, ed. Emilie M. Townes (Maryknoll, N.Y.: Orbis Books, 1997), 161.

8. The idea of sin that oppresses black women in a given church community may only be informal theology, but the idea is still just as effective in excluding or condemning women. "In the sacred world of black Baptist

and Methodist denominations, women are confronted with the ideologies of the Pauline epistles, women's physical inability to preach in a
dramatic, energetic, and celebrative style, or the problems posed by preg-
nancy. In a world where 'the call' is seen as something reserved strictly
for men, black women preachers are sharply and persistently questioned"
(Cheryl Townsend Gilkes, "The Roles of Church and Community Mothers: Ambivalent American Sexism or Fragmented African Familyhood?"
in *African-American Religion: Interpretive Essays in History and Culture*,
ed. Timothy E. Fulop and Albert J. Raboteau [New York: Routledge,
1997], 381).

9. Sheron C. Patterson, *New Faith: A Black Christian Woman's Guide
to Reformation, Re-creation, Rediscovery, Renaissance, Resurrection, and
Revival* (Minneapolis: Fortress Press, 2000), 26.

10. Delores Williams, "A Womanist Perspective on Sin," in *A Troubling
in My Soul,* 137–38.

11. Ibid., 144.

12. Ibid., 147.

13. Ibid.

14. Jacquelyn Grant, "The Sin of Servanthood and the Deliverance of
Discipleship," in *A Troubling in My Soul,* 212.

15. Ibid., 213.

16. Ibid., 216.

17. Delores S. Williams, *Sisters in the Wilderness: The Challenge of
Womanist God-Talk* (Maryknoll, N.Y.: Orbis Books, 1993), 167.

18. Cited in Grace Jordan McFadden, "Septima P. Clark and the
Struggle for Human Rights," in *This Far by Faith: Readings in African-
American Women's Religious Biography,* ed. Judith Weisenfeld and
Richard Newman (New York: Routledge, 1996), 308.

19. Jacquelyn Grant, "Womanist Jesus and the Mutual Struggle for
Liberation," in *The Recovery of Black Presence,* 129.

20. Delores Williams, "Straight Talk, Plain Talk: Womanist Words
about Salvation in a Social Context," in *Embracing the Spirit,* 97–121.

21. Ibid., 119.

22. Grant, "Womanist Theology," 217.

23. For a detailed discussion, see Grant, "Womanist Jesus," 131–38.

24. Kelly Brown Douglas, *The Black Christ* (Maryknoll, N.Y.: Orbis
Books, 1994).

25. Ibid., 78.

26. Ibid., 107.

27. Ibid., 112.

28. Ibid., 111.

29. Williams, *Sisters in the Wilderness,* 167.

30. Ibid., 168.

31. JoAnne Marie Terrell, *Power in the Blood: The Cross in the African American Experience* (Maryknoll, N.Y.: Orbis Books, 1998), 120.

32. Ibid., 142.

33. Ibid., 124–25.

34. Grant, *White Women's Christ*, 211.

35. Williams, *Sisters in the Wilderness*, 219–34.

36. Ibid., 149.

37. Randall C. Bailey, "Academic Biblical Interpretation among African Americans in the United States," in *African Americans and the Bible: Sacred Texts and Social Textures*, ed. Vincent L. Wimbush (New York: Continuum, 2001), 707.

38. Vincent L. Wimbush, "Reading Scriptures, Reading Darkness," in *African Americans and the Bible*, 9.

39. Diana L. Hayes, *And Still We Rise: An Introduction to Black Liberation Theology* (Mahwah, N.J.: Paulist Press, 1996), 98.

40. For example, see Clifton H. Johnson, ed., *God Struck Me Dead: Voices of Ex-Slaves* (Cleveland: Pilgrim Press, 1993).

41. Such as several women reported in Dorothy L. Pennington, *African American Women Quitting the Workplace* (Lewiston, N.Y.: Edwin Mellen Press, 1999).

42. Karen Baker-Fletcher and Garth Baker-Fletcher, *My Sister, My Brother: Womanist and Xodus God-Talk* (Maryknoll, N.Y.: Orbis Books, 1997), 27.

43. Ibid., 39.

44. Ibid., 36.

45. Ibid., 28.

46. Cheryl Kirk-Duggan, *Refiner's Fire: Religious Engagement with Violence* (Minneapolis: Fortress Press, 2001), 157.

47. Ibid.

48. For discussion on gendered God-language among African American women, see Williams, *Sisters in the Wilderness*, 56.

49. Patterson, *New Faith*, 29.

50. Diana L. Hayes, *Hagar's Daughters: Womanist Ways of Being in the World* (New York: Paulist Press, 1995), 54.

51. Karen Baker-Fletcher, *A Singing Something: Womanist Reflections on Anna Julia Cooper* (New York: Crossroad, 1994), 108.

52. Ibid., 188–206.

53. Ibid., 197.

54. Ibid., 204.

55. Ibid., 205.

56. Diana L. Hayes, "My Hope Is in the Lord: Transformation and Salvation in the African American Community," in *Embracing the Spirit*, 23.

Chapter 7: New Challenges, Lingering Questions

1. Teresa L. Fry Brown, "Avoiding Asphyxiation: A Womanist Perspective in Intrapersonal and Interpersonal Transformation," in *Embracing the Spirit: Womanist Perspectives on Hope, Salvation, and Transformation,* ed. Emilie M. Townes (Maryknoll, N.Y.: Orbis Books, 1997), 76.

2. Marsha Foster Boyd, "WomanistCare: Some Reflections on the Pastoral Care and the Transformation of African American Women," in *Embracing the Spirit,* 197–202.

3. Ibid., 198.

4. Carroll A. Watkins Ali, *Survival and Liberation: Pastoral Theology in African American Context* (St. Louis: Chalice Press, 1999), 8.

5. Ibid., 110–18.

6. Ibid., 121.

7. Yolanda Y. Smith, unpublished paper presented at American Academy of Religion/Lilly Foundation, conference titled Mining the Motherlode of African American Religious Life, February 2000.

8. Cheryl Kirk-Duggan, *African American Special Days: 15 Complete Worship Services* (Nashville: Abingdon Press, 1996).

9. Patricia L. Hunter, "Women's Power, Women's Passion: And God Said, 'That's Good,' " in *A Troubling in My Soul: Womanist Perspectives on Evil and Suffering,* ed. Emilie M. Townes (Maryknoll, N.Y.: Orbis Books, 1993), 193.

10. Ibid., 198.

11. Karen Baker-Fletcher and Garth Baker-Fletcher, *My Sister, My Brother: Womanist and Xodus God-Talk* (Maryknoll, N.Y.: Orbis Books, 1997), 245.

12. Emilie M. Townes, *In a Blaze of Glory: Womanist Spirituality as Social Witness* (Nashville: Abingdon Press, 1995), 140–44.

13. Evelyn Brooks Higginbotham, *Righteous Discontent: The Women's Movement in the Black Baptist Church, 1880–1920* (Cambridge, Mass.: Harvard University Press, 1993), 7.

14. Gayraud S. Wilmore, *Black Religion and Black Radicalism: An Interpretation of the Religious History of Afro-American People* (Maryknoll, N.Y.: Orbis Books, 1993), "Deradicalization of the Black Church," 135–66, and "Dechristianization of Black Radicalism," 167–91.

15. Taylor Branch, *Parting the Waters: America in the King Years 1954–1963* (New York: Simon and Schuster, 1988).

16. Delores S. Williams, *Sisters in the Wilderness: The Challenge of Womanist God-Talk* (Maryknoll, N.Y.: Orbis Books, 1993), 207–9.

17. Diana L. Hayes, *And Still We Rise: An Introduction to Black Liberation Theology* (Mahwah, N.J.: Paulist Press, 1996), 161.

18. See her essay on one expression of the Muslim faith among African Americans: Debra Washington Mubashshir, "Forgotten Fruit of the City: Chicago and the Moorish Science Temple of America," in *CrossCurrents* 51, no. 1 (spring 2001): 6–20.

19. Stuart Hall, "Subjects in History: Making Diasporic Identities," in *The House That Race Built: Black Americans, U.S. Terrain,* ed. Wahneema Lubiano (New York: Pantheon Books, 1997), 292.

20. Sidney Lemelle and Robin D. G. Kelley, eds., *Imagining Home: Class, Culture, and Nationalism in the African Diaspora* (London: Verso, 1994), 7.

21. Alice Eley Jones, "Sacred Places and Holy Ground: West African Spiritualism at Stagville Plantation," in *Keep Your Head to the Sky: Interpreting African American Home Ground,* ed. Grey Gundaker (Charlottesville: University Press of Virginia, 1998), 95.

22. Ibid., 101.

23. These explorations include personal journeys to traditional African beliefs, such as found in the autobiographical account of Malidoma Patrice Some, *Of Water and Spirit: Ritual, Magic, and Initiation in the Life of an African Shaman* (New York: G. P. Putnam's Sons, 1994).

24. Zora Neale Hurston, *The Sanctified Church* (Berkeley, Calif.: Turtle Island Press, 1981).

25. Harold Courlander, *A Treasury of Afro-American Folklore* (New York: Smithmark Publishers, 1996), 2.

26. Michael L. Blakely, "The New York African Burial Project: An Examination of Enslaved Lives," *Transforming Anthropology: Journal of the Association of Black Anthropologists* 7, no. 1 (1998): 53–58.

27. Sheila Turnage, "Saving the Dead," *American Legacy* (fall 1998): 59–64.

28. Carolyn C. Denard, "Retrieving and Reappropriating the Values of the Black Church Tradition through Written Narratives," in *The Stones That the Builders Rejected: The Development of Ethical Leadership from the Black Church Tradition,* ed. Walter Earl Fluker (Harrisburg, Pa.: Trinity Press International, 1998), 82.

29. Joan M. Martin, *More Than Chains and Toil: A Christian Work Ethic of Enslaved Women* (Louisville: Westminster John Knox Press, 2000), 150.

30. Peter J. Paris, *The Spirituality of African Peoples: The Search for a Common Moral Discourse* (Minneapolis: Fortress Press, 1995).

31. Ibid., 33–48.

32. Townes, *In a Blaze of Glory,* 22.

33. Rachel E. Harding, *A Refuge in Thunder: Candomblé and Alternative Spaces of Blackness* (Bloomington: Indiana University Press, 2000).

34. Baker-Fletcher and Baker-Fletcher, *My Sister, My Brother*, 89, 90.

35. Ibid., 91.

36. Carolyn McCrary, "Interdependence as a Normative Value in Pastoral Counseling with African Americans," in *The Recovery of Black Presence: An Interdisciplinary Exploration,* ed. Randall C. Bailey and Jacquelyn Grant (Nashville: Abingdon Press, 1995), 161–63.

37. Iyanla Vanzant, *The Value in the Valley: A Black Woman's Guide through Life's Dilemmas* (New York: Simon and Schuster, 1995).

38. Toinette M. Eugene, "Swing Low, Sweet Chariot: A Womanist Response to Sexual Violence and Abuse," *Daughters of Sarah* 20 no. 3 (summer 1994): 10–13; and Eugene, "Walking in the Light: A Womanist Ethical Response to the Questions about Domestic Violence, 'Where Do We Go from Here?' " (paper presented at New York Theological Seminary, March 3–4, 1995).

39. Toinette M. Eugene, "While Love Is Unfashionable: Ethical Implications of Black Spirituality and Sexuality," in *Feminist Ethics and the Catholic Moral Tradition,* Readings in Moral Theology, no. 9, ed. Charles E. Curran, Margaret A. Farley, and Richard A. McCormick, S.J. (Mahwah, N.J.: Paulist Press, 1996), 316.

40. Ibid., 318.

41. Kelly Brown Douglas, *Sexuality and the Black Church: A Womanist Perspective* (Maryknoll, N.Y.: Orbis Books, 1999), 128.

42. Ibid., 142.

43. Ibid., 120.

44. Williams, *Sisters in the Wilderness,* 209.

45. Hurston, *The Sanctified Church.*

46. Ruth Landes, *The City of Women* (Albuquerque: University of New Mexico Press, 1994).

47. Renato Rosaldo, *Culture and Truth: The Remaking of Social Analysis* (Boston: Beacon Press, 1989), 194.

48. Linda E. Thomas, "Womanist Theology, Epistemology, and a New Anthropological Paradigm," *CrossCurrents* 48 (winter 1998): 495.

49. Ibid., 496.

50. Cheryl Townsend Gilkes, " 'A Conscious Connection to All That Is': *The Color Purple* as Subversive and Critical Ethnography," in *Embracing the Spirit,* 276–77.

51. For information, contact the African Atlantic Research Team, Department of Ethnic Studies, 30 Ketchum, Boulder, CO 80309.

52. Thomas, "Womanist Theology," 492.

Bibliography

Ali, Carroll A. Watkins. *Survival and Liberation: Pastoral Theology in African American Context.* St. Louis: Chalice Press, 1999.

Anderson, Victor. *Beyond Ontological Blackness: An Essay on African American Religious and Cultural Criticism.* New York: Continuum, 1995.

Andolsen, Barbara Hilkert. *Daughters of Jefferson, Daughters of Bootblacks: Racism and American Feminism.* Macon, Ga.: Mercer University Press, 1986.

Austin, Denise A. "Aunt Hagar's Daughters: Three Women in the Neo-Pentecostal Tradition." In *Nature of a Sistuh: Black Women's Lived Experiences in Contemporary Culture,* edited by T. McDonald and T. Ford-Ahmed, 169–82. Durham, N.C.: Carolina Academic Press, 1999.

Bailey, Randall C. "Academic Biblical Interpretation among African Americans in the United States." In *African Americans and the Bible: Sacred Texts and Social Textures,* edited by Vincent L. Wimbush, 696–711. New York: Continuum, 2001.

Baker-Fletcher, Garth Kasimu. *Xodus: An African American Male Journey.* Minneapolis: Fortress Press, 1996.

Baker-Fletcher, Karen. *A Singing Something: Womanist Reflections on Anna Julia Cooper.* New York: Crossroad, 1994.

Baker-Fletcher, Karen, and Garth Baker-Fletcher. *My Sister, My Brother: Womanist and Xodus God-Talk.* Maryknoll, N.Y.: Orbis Books, 1997.

Bell, Yvonne R., Cathy L. Bouie, and Joseph Baldwin. "Afrocentric Cultural Consciousness and African American Male-Female Relationships." In *Afrocentric Visions: Studies in Culture and Communication,* edited by Janice D. Hamlet, 47–72. Thousand Oaks, Calif.: Sage Publications, 1998.

Blakely, Michael L. "The New York African Burial Project: An Examination of Enslaved Lives." *Transforming Anthropology: Journal of the Association of Black Anthropologists* 7, no. 1 (1998): 53–58.

Boyce Davies, Carol. "Mothering and Healing in Recent Black Women's Fiction." *Sage* 2, no. 1 (spring 1985): 41–43.

Boyd, Marsha Foster. "WomanistCare: Some Reflections on the Pastoral Care and the Transformation of African American Women." In *Embracing the Spirit: Womanist Perspectives on Hope, Salvation, and Transformation*, edited by Emilie M. Townes, 197–202. Maryknoll, N.Y.: Orbis Books, 1997.

Branch, Taylor. *Parting the Waters: America in the King Years 1954–1963.* New York: Simon and Schuster Inc., 1988.

Bridges, Donyale. Unpublished paper, June 2000.

Brown, Teresa L. Fry. "Avoiding Asphyxiation: A Womanist Perspective in Intrapersonal and Interpersonal Transformation." In *Embracing the Spirit: Womanist Perspectives on Hope, Salvation, and Transformation,* edited by Emilie M. Townes, 72–94. Maryknoll, N.Y.: Orbis Books, 1997.

Burbridge, Lynn C. "Black Women in the History of African American Economic Thought: A Critical Essay." In *A Different Vision: African American Economic Thought,* edited by T. Boston. Vol. 1, 101–22. New York: Routledge, 1997.

Cannon, Katie G. *Black Womanist Ethics*. Atlanta: Scholars Press, 1988.

———. *Katie's Canon: Womanism and the Soul of the Black Community.* New York: Continuum, 1995.

———. "Womanist Interpretation and Preaching in the Black Church." In *Searching the Scriptures: A Feminist Introduction,* edited by Elisabeth Schüssler Fiorenza, 326–37. New York: Crossroad, 1993.

Carby, Hazel V. *Race Men*. Cambridge, Mass.: Harvard University Press, 1998.

———. *Reconstructing Womanhood: The Emergence of the Afro-American Woman Novelist.* New York: Oxford University Press, 1987.

Chowdhury, Kanishka. "Afrocentric Voices: Constructing Identities, (Dis)-Placing Difference." In *Race-ing Representation: Voice, History, and Sexuality,* edited by K. Myrsiades and L. Myrsiades, 17–41. Lanham, Md.: Rowan and Littlefield Publishers, 1998.

Chung Hyun Kyung. *Struggle to Be the Sun Again: Introducing Asian Women's Theology.* Maryknoll, N.Y.: Orbis Books, 1990.

Coleman, Will. *Tribal Talk: Black Theology, Hermeneutics, and African/American Ways of "Telling the Story."* University Park: University of Pennsylvania Press, 2000.

Collins, Patricia Hill. *Black Feminist Thought: Knowledge, Consciousness, and the Politics of Empowerment.* New York: Routledge, 1990.

———. *Fighting Words: Black Women and the Search for Justice.* Minneapolis: University of Minnesota Press, 1998.

Cone, James H. *Black Theology and Black Power.* New York: Seabury Press, 1969.

———. "Looking Back, Going Forward: Black Theology as Public Theology." In *Black Faith and Public Talk: Critical Essays on James H. Cone's "Black Theology and Black Power,"* edited by Dwight N. Hopkins, 246–60. Maryknoll, N.Y.: Orbis Books, 1999.

———. *Risks of Faith: The Emergence of a Black Theology of Liberation, 1968–1998.* Boston: Beacon Press, 1999.

Copeland, M. Shawn. "Wading through Many Sorrows: Toward a Theology of Suffering in Womanist Perspective." In *A Troubling in My Soul: Womanist Perspectives on Evil and Suffering,* edited by Emilie M. Townes, 109–29. Maryknoll, N.Y.: Orbis Books, 1993.

Courlander, Harold. *A Treasury of Afro-American Folklore.* New York: Smithmark Publishers, 1996.

Cummings, Lorine. "A Womanist Response to the Afrocentric Idea: Jarena Lee, Womanist Preacher." In *Living the Intersection: Womanism and Afrocentrism in Theology,* edited by Cheryl Sanders, 57–64. Minneapolis: Fortress Press, 1995.

Denard, Carolyn C. "Retrieving and Reappropriating the Values of the Black Church Tradition through Written Narratives." In *The Stones That the Builders Rejected: The Development of Ethical Leadership from the Black Church Tradition,* edited by Walter Earl Fluker, 82–96. Harrisburg, Pa.: Trinity Press International, 1998.

Douglas, Kelly Brown. *The Black Christ.* Maryknoll, N.Y.: Orbis Books, 1994.

———. "To Reflect the Image of God: A Womanist Perspective on Right Relationship." In *Living the Intersection: Womanism and Afrocentrism in Theology,* edited by Cheryl J. Sanders, 67–77. Minneapolis: Fortress Press, 1995.

———. *Sexuality and the Black Church: A Womanist Perspective.* Maryknoll, N.Y.: Orbis Books, 1999.

———. "Teaching Womanist Theology." In *Living the Intersection: Womanism and Afrocentrism in Theology,* edited by Cheryl J. Sanders, 147–56. Minneapolis: Fortress Press, 1995.

Ekeya, Bette. "Woman, for How Long Not?" In *Feminist Theology from the Third World: A Reader,* edited by Ursula King, 139–49. Maryknoll, N.Y.: Orbis Books, 1995.

Eneme, Grace. "Women as Living Stones." In *Feminist Theology from the Third World: A Reader,* edited by Ursula King, 214–19. Maryknoll, N.Y.: Orbis Books, 1995.

Erskine, Noel L. *Decolonizing Theology: A Caribbean Perspective.* Maryknoll, N.Y.: Orbis Books, 1981.

Essed, Philomena. *Understanding Everyday Racism: An Interdisciplinary Theory.* Newbury Park, Calif.: Sage Publications, 1991.

Essex, Barbara. "Some Kind of Woman." In *Embracing the Spirit: Womanist Perspectives on Hope, Salvation, and Transformation,* edited by Emilie M. Townes, 203–11. Maryknoll, N.Y.: Orbis Books, 1997.

Eugene, Toinette M. "Moral Values and Black Womanists." *Journal of Religious Thought* 44 (winter–spring 1988): 23–34.

———. "Regardless: An Attitude of Being for Women under Fire." *Update: Newsletter of the Evangelical and Ecumenical Women's Caucus* 14, no. 3 (winter 1990/91): 23–34.

———. "Swing Low, Sweet Chariot: A Womanist Response to Sexual Violence and Abuse." *Daughters of Sarah* 20, no. 3 (summer 1994): 10–13.

———. "Walking in the Light: A Womanist Ethical Response to the Questions about Domestic Violence, 'Where Do We Go from Here?'" Paper presented March 3–4, 1995, New York Theological Seminary.

———. "While Love Is Unfashionable: Ethical Implications of Black Spirituality and Sexuality." In *Feminist Ethics and the Catholic Moral Tradition,* edited by Charles E. Curran, Margaret A. Farley, and Richard A. McCormick, S.J., 315–37. Readings in Moral Theology, no. 9. Mahwah, N.J.: Paulist Press, 1996.

Fabella, Virginia, M.M., and R. S. Sugirtharajah, eds. *Dictionary of Third World Theologies.* Maryknoll, N.Y.: Orbis Books, 2000.

Fiorenza, Elisabeth Schüssler. "Transforming the Legacy of *The Woman's Bible.*" In *Searching the Scriptures: A Feminist Introduction,* vol. 1, edited by Elisabeth Schüssler Fiorenza, 1–24. New York: Crossroad, 1993.

Fluker, Walter E., and Catherine Tumber, eds. *A Strange Freedom: The Best of Howard Thurman on Religious Experience and Public Life.* Boston: Beacon Press, 1998.

Gebara, Ivone. "Women Doing Theology in Latin America." In *Feminist Theology from the Third World,* edited by Ursula King, 47–59. Maryknoll, N.Y.: Orbis Books, 1994.

Giddings, Paula. *When and Where I Enter: The Impact of Black Women on Race and Sex in America.* New York: Bantam Books, 1984.

Gilkes, Cheryl Townsend. "'A Conscious Connection to All That Is': *The Color Purple* as Subversive and Critical Ethnography." In *Embracing the Spirit: Womanist Perspectives on Hope, Salvation, and Transformation,* edited by Emilie M. Townes, 275–96. Maryknoll, N.Y.: Orbis Books, 1997.

———. *If It Wasn't for the Women.* Maryknoll, N.Y.: Orbis Books, 2001.

————. "The Loves and Troubles of African-American Women's Bodies: The Womanist Challenge to Cultural Humiliation and Community Ambivalence." In *A Troubling in My Soul: Womanist Perspectives on Evil and Suffering*, edited by Emilie M. Townes, 239–40. Maryknoll, N.Y.: Orbis Books, 1993.

————. "The Roles of Church and Community Mothers: Ambivalent American Sexism or Fragmented African Familyhood?" In *African-American Religion: Interpretive Essays in History and Culture*, edited by Timothy E. Fulop and Albert J. Raboteau, 365–88. N.Y.: Routledge, 1997.

————. " 'Some Mother's Son and Some Father's Daughter': Gender and Biblical Language in Afro-Christian Worship Tradition." In *Shaping New Visions: Gender and Values in American Culture*, edited by Clarissa W. Atkinson, Constance Hall Buchanan, and Margaret R. Miles, 73–99. Ann Arbor, Mich.: UMI Research Press, 1987.

Gilroy, Paul. *The Black Atlantic: Modernity and Double Consciousness*. Cambridge, Mass.: Harvard University Press, 1993.

Grant, Jacquelyn. "Servanthood Revisited: Womanist Explorations of Servanthood Theology." In *Black Faith and Public Talk: Critical Essays on James H. Cone's "Black Theology and Black Power,"* edited by Dwight Hopkins, 127–37. Maryknoll, N.Y.: Orbis Books, 1999.

————. "The Sin of Servanthood and the Deliverance of Discipleship." In *A Troubling in My Soul: Womanist Perspectives on Evil and Suffering*, edited by Emilie M. Townes, 199–218. Maryknoll, N.Y.: Orbis Books, 1993.

————. *White Women's Christ, Black Women's Jesus: Feminist Christology and Womanist Response*. Atlanta: Scholars Press, 1989.

————. "Womanist Jesus and the Mutual Struggle for Liberation." In *The Recovery of Black Presence*, edited by Randall C. Bailey and Jacquelyn Grant, 129–42. Nashville: Abingdon Press, 1995.

————. "Womanist Theology: Black Women's Experience as a Source for Doing Theology, with Special Reference to Christology." In *African American Religious Studies: An Interdisciplinary Anthology*, edited by Gayraud Wilmore, 208–26. Durham, N.C.: Duke University Press, 1989.

Hacker, Andrew. *Two Nations: Black and White, Separate, Hostile, Unequal*. New York: Charles Scribner's Sons, 1992.

Hall, Stuart. "Subjects in History: Making Diasporic Identities." In *The House That Race Built: Black Americans, U.S. Terrain*, edited by Wahneema Lubiano, 289–99. New York: Pantheon Books, 1997.

Harding, Rachel E. *A Refuge in Thunder: Candomblé and Alternative Spaces of Blackness*. Bloomington: Indiana University Press, 2000.

Hayes, Diana L. *Hagar's Daughters: Womanist Ways of Being in the World.* Mahwah, N.J.: Paulist Press, 1995.

———. "My Hope Is in the Lord: Transformation and Salvation in the African American Community." In *Embracing the Spirit: Womanist Perspectives on Hope, Salvation, and Transformation,* edited by Emilie M. Townes, 9–28. Maryknoll, N.Y.: Orbis Books, 1997.

———. *And Still We Rise: An Introduction to Black Liberation Theology.* Mahwah, N.J.: Paulist Press, 1996.

Higginbotham, Evelyn Brooks. "African American Women's History and the Metalanguage of Race." In *"We Specialize in the Wholly Impossible": A Reader in Black Women's History,* edited by Darlene Clark Hine, Wilma King, and Linda Reed, 3–24. Brooklyn, N.Y.: Carlson Publishing, 1995.

———. *Righteous Discontent: The Women's Movement in the Black Baptist Church, 1880–1920.* Cambridge, Mass.: Harvard University Press, 1993.

Hine, Darlene Clark. *Black Women in American History.* Vols. 1–16. Brooklyn, N.Y.: Carlson Publishing, 1990.

———. *Hine Sight: Black Women and the Re-construction of American History.* Brooklyn, N.Y.: Carlson Publishing, 1994.

Hine, Darlene Clark, Wilma King, and Linda Reed, eds. *"We Specialize in the Wholly Impossible": A Reader in Black Women's History.* Brooklyn, N.Y.: Carlson Publishing, 1995.

Hoffnar, Emily, and Michael Greene. "Residential Location and the Earnings of African American Women." In *African Americans and Post-industrial Labor Markets,* edited by J. B. Stewart, 237–46. New Brunswick, N.J.: Transaction Publishers, 1997.

Hood, Robert E. *Begrimed and Black: Christian Traditions on Blacks and Blackness.* Minneapolis: Fortress Press, 1994.

hooks, bell. *Sisters of the Yam: Black Women, and Self-Recovery.* Boston: South End Press, 1993.

———. *Teaching to Transgress: Education as the Practice of Freedom.* New York: Routledge, 1994.

———. *Where We Stand: Class Matters.* New York: Routledge, 2000.

Hopkins, Dwight N. *Introducing Black Theology of Liberation.* Maryknoll, N.Y.: Orbis Books, 1999.

Hunter, Patricia L. "Women's Power, Women's Passion: And God Said, 'That's Good.'" In *A Troubling in My Soul: Womanist Perspectives on Evil and Suffering,* edited by Emilie M. Townes, 189–98. Maryknoll, N.Y.: Orbis Books, 1993.

Hurmence, Belinda, ed. *My Folks Don't Want Me to Talk about Slavery: Twenty-One Oral Histories of Former North Carolina Slaves.* Winston-Salem, N.C.: John F. Blair, 1984.

Hurston, Zora Neale. *The Sanctified Church.* Berkeley, Calif.: Turtle Island Press, 1981.

James, James Ella. "It's How the Women 'Read' Their 'Titles Clear.' " In *African Americans and the Bible: Sacred Texts and Social Textures,* edited by Vincent L. Wimbush, 840–43. New York: Continuum, 2001.

James, Joy. *Shadowboxing: Representations of Black Feminist Politics.* New York: St. Martin's Press, 1999.

———. *Transcending the Talented Tenth: Black Leaders and American Intellectuals.* New York: Routledge, 1997.

James, Stanlie M., and Abena P. A. Busia, eds. *Theorizing Black Feminisms: The Visionary Pragmatism of Black Feminisms.* New York: Routledge, 1993.

James, Valerie E. Unpublished paper, November 2001.

Johnson, Clifton H. *God Struck Me Dead: Voices of Ex-Slaves.* Cleveland: Pilgrim Press, 1993.

Jones, Alice Eley. "Sacred Places and Holy Ground: West African Spiritualism at Stagville Plantation." In *Keep Your Head to the Sky: Interpreting African American Home Ground,* edited by Grey Gundaker, 93–109. Charlottesville: University Press of Virginia, 1998.

Juster, Susan, and Lisa MacFarlane, eds. *A Mighty Baptism: Race, Gender, and the Creation of American Protestantism.* Ithaca, N.Y.: Cornell University Press, 1996.

Kalof, Linda, and Bruce Wade. "Sexual Attitudes and Experiences with Sexual Coercion: Exploring the Influence of Race and Gender." *Journal of Black Psychology* 21, no. 3 (August 1995): 236–41.

Karenga, Maulana. *Introduction to Black Studies.* 3d ed. Los Angeles: University of Sankore Press, 2002.

King, Ursula, ed. *Feminist Theology from the Third World: A Reader.* Maryknoll, N.Y.: Orbis Books, 1995.

Kirk-Duggan, Cheryl A. *African American Special Days: 15 Complete Worship Services.* Nashville: Abingdon Press, 1996.

———. *Exorcising Evil: A Womanist Perspective on the Spirituals.* Maryknoll, N.Y.: Orbis Books, 1997.

———. "Justified, Sanctified, and Redeemed: Blessed Expectation in Black Women's Blues and Gospels." In *Embracing the Spirit: Womanist Perspectives on Hope, Salvation, and Transformation,* edited by Emilie M. Townes, 140–66. Maryknoll, N.Y.: Orbis Books, 1997.

————. *Misbegotten Anguish: A Theology and Ethics of Violence.* St. Louis: Chalice Press, 2001.

————. *Refiner's Fire: Religious Engagement with Violence.* Minneapolis: Fortress Press, 2001.

Landes, Ruth. *The City of Women.* Albuquerque: University of New Mexico Press, 1994.

Lemelle, Sidney, and Robin D. G. Kelley, eds. *Imagining Home: Class, Culture, and Nationalism in the African Diaspora.* London: Verso, 1994.

Lemke-Santangelo, Gretchen. *Abiding Courage: African American Migrant Women and the East Bay Community.* Chapel Hill: University of North Carolina Press, 1996.

Lerner, Gerda, ed. *Black Women in White America: A Documentary History.* New York: Vintage Books, 1973.

Levine, Lawrence W. *Black Culture and Black Consciousness: Afro-American Folk Thought from Slavery to Freedom.* New York: Oxford University Press, 1977.

Mack, Kibibi V. C. *Parlor Ladies and Ebony Drudges: African American Women, Class, and Work in a South Carolina Community.* Nashville: University of Tennessee Press, 1999.

Martin, Joan M. *More Than Chains or Toil: A Christian Work Ethic of Enslaved Women.* Louisville: Westminster John Knox Press, 2000.

Mbiti, John S. *African Religions and Philosophy.* New York: Anchor Books, 1970.

McCrary, Carolyn. "Interdependence as a Normative Value in Pastoral Counseling with African Americans." In *The Recovery of Black Presence: An Interdisciplinary Exploration,* edited by Randall C. Bailey and Jacquelyn Grant, 159–76. Nashville: Abingdon Press, 1995.

McDonald, Trevy, and T. Ford-Ahmed. *Nature of a Sistuh: Black Women's Lived Experiences in Contemporary Culture.* Durham, N.C.: Carolina Academic Press, 1999.

McFadden, Grace Jordan. "Septima P. Clark and the Struggle for Human Rights." In *This Far by Faith: Readings in African-American Women's Religious Biography,* edited by Judith Weisenfeld and Richard Newman, 300–312. New York: Routledge, 1996.

Meltzer, Milton. *In Their Own Words: A History of the American Negro.* New York: Apollo Editions, 1965.

Miller-McLemore, Bonnie J., and B. Gill-Austern, eds. *Feminist and Womanist Pastoral Theology.* Nashville: Abingdon Books, 1999.

Mintz, Sidney W., and Richard Price. *The Birth of African American Culture: An Anthropological Perspective.* Boston: Beacon Press, 1976 (preface 1992).

Mitchem, Stephanie Y. *Getting Off the Cross: African American Women, Health, and Salvation.* Ann Arbor, Mich.: UMI Dissertation Services, 1998.

Montilius, Guerin. *Dompim: The Spirituality of African Peoples.* Nashville: Winston-Derek Publishers, 1989.

Mubashshir, Debra Washington. "Forgotten Fruit of the City: Chicago and the Moorish Science Temple of America." *CrossCurrents* 51, no. 1 (spring 2001): 6–20.

Mullings, Leith. *On Our Own Terms: Race, Class, and Gender in the Lives of African American Women.* New York: Routledge, 1997.

Oduyoye, Mercy Amba. *Daughters of Anowa: African Women and Patriarchy.* Maryknoll, N.Y.: Orbis Books, 1995.

———. *Hearing and Knowing: Theological Reflections on Christianity in Africa.* Maryknoll, N.Y.: Orbis, 1986.

Oduyoye, Mercy Amba, and Musimbi R. A. Kanyoro, eds. *The Will to Arise: Women, Tradition, and the Church in Africa.* Maryknoll, N.Y.: Orbis Books, 1992.

Oduyoye, Mercy Amba, and Roina Fa'atauva'a. "The Struggle about Women's Theological Education." In *Feminist Theology from the Third World: A Reader,* edited by Ursula King, 170–76. Maryknoll, N.Y.: Orbis Books, 1995.

Paris, Peter J. *The Spirituality of African Peoples: The Search for a Common Moral Discourse.* Minneapolis: Fortress Press, 1995.

Patterson, Sheron C. *New Faith: A Black Christian Woman's Guide to Reformation, Re-creation, Rediscovery, Renaissance, Resurrection, and Revival.* Minneapolis: Fortress Press, 2000.

Pedraja, Luis. *Jesus Is My Uncle: Christology from a Hispanic Perspective.* Nashville: Abingdon Press, 1999.

Pennington Dorothy L. *African American Women Quitting the Workplace.* Lewiston, N.Y.: Edwin Mellen Press, 1999.

Peterson, Carla F. *"Doers of the Word": African American Women Speakers and Writers in the North, 1830–1880.* New York: Oxford University Press, 1995.

Raboteau, Albert. "The Afro-American Traditions." In *Caring and Curing: Health and Medicine in the Western Religious Traditions,* edited by Ronald L. Numbers and Darrel W. Amundsen, 539–62. New York: Macmillan Publishing Co., 1986.

———. *Canaan Land: A Religious History of African Americans.* New York: Oxford University Press, 2001.

Ratcliff, Carolyn. Unpublished paper, June 2000.

Reed, Adolph, Jr. *Class Notes: Posing as Politics and Other Thoughts on the American Scene.* New York: New Press, 2000.

Richie, Beth. *Compelled to Crime: The Gender Entrapment of Battered Black Women.* New York: Routledge, 1996.

Riggs, Marcia. *Awake, Arise, and Act: A Womanist Call for Black Liberation.* Cleveland: Pilgrim Press, 1994.

———. *Can I Get a Witness? Prophetic Religious Voices of African American Women.* Maryknoll, N.Y.: Orbis Books, 1997.

Roberts, Dorothy. *Killing the Black Body: Race, Reproduction, and the Meaning of Liberty.* New York: Pantheon Books, 1997.

———. "The Value of Black Mothers' Work." *Radical America* 26, no. 1 (1996): 9–16.

Romero, Mary, and Debbie Storrs. " 'Is That Sociology?' The Accounts of Women of Color Graduate Students in Ph.D. Programs." In *Women Leading in Education,* edited by Diane M. Dunlap and Patrick A. Schmuck. Albany: State University of New York Press, 1995.

Rosaldo, Renato. *Culture and Truth: The Remaking of Social Analysis.* Boston: Beacon Press, 1989.

Rouson, Brigette. "Journeys in African-American Womanhood: Emerging Community-Oriented Spirituality." In *Nature of a Sistuh: Black Women's Lived Experiences in Contemporary Culture,* edited by Trevy McDonald and T. Ford-Ahmed, 145–68. Durham, N.C.: Carolina Academic Press, 1999.

Schechter, Patricia A. " 'All the Intensity of My Nature': Ida B. Wells, Anger, and Politics." *Radical History Review* 70 (winter 1998): 48–77.

Simpson, George Eaton. *Black Religion in the New World.* New York: Columbia University Press, 1978.

Smith, Rogers M. "Toward a More Perfect Union: Beyond Old Liberalism and Neoliberalism." In *Without Justice for All,* edited by Adolph Reed Jr., 327–52. Boulder, Colo.: Westview Press, 1999.

Smith, Susan L. *Sick and Tired of Being Sick and Tired: Black Women's Health Activism in America, 1890–1950.* Philadelphia: University of Pennsylvania Press, 1995.

Smith, Yolanda Y. Unpublished paper presented at American Academy of Religion/Lilly Foundation, conference titled Mining the Motherlode of African American Religious Life. February 2000.

Some, Malidoma Patrice. *Of Water and Spirit: Ritual, Magic, and Initiation in the Life of an African Shaman.* New York: G. P. Putnam's Sons, 1994.

Stampp, Kenneth. *The Peculiar Institution: Slavery in the Antebellum South.* New York: Vintage Books, 1955.

Steinberg, Steven. "The Liberal Retreat from Race during the Post–Civil Rights Era." In *The House That Race Built: Black Americans, U.S.*

Terrain, edited by Wahneema Lubiano, 13–47. New York: Pantheon Books, 1997.

Stuckey, Sterling. *Slave Culture: Nationalist Theory and the Foundations of Black America*. New York: Oxford University Press, 1987.

Terborg-Penn, Rosalyn. *African American Women in the Struggle for the Vote, 1850–1920*. Bloomington: Indiana University Press, 1998.

Terrell, JoAnne Marie. *Power in the Blood: The Cross in the African American Experience*. Maryknoll, N.Y.: Orbis Books, 1998.

Thomas, Linda E. "Emancipatory Christianity." In *Black Faith and Public Talk: Critical Essays on James H. Cone's "Black Theology and Black Power,"* edited by Dwight N. Hopkins, 178–89. Maryknoll, N.Y.: Orbis Books, 1999.

———. "Womanist Theology, Epistemology, and a New Anthropological Paradigm." *CrossCurrents* 48 (winter 1998): 488–99.

Thompson, Kathleen, and Hilary MacAustin. *The Face of Our Past: Images of Black Women from Colonial America to the Present*. Bloomington: Indiana University Press, 1999.

Tillman, Janice N. Unpublished paper, June 2000.

Townes, Emilie M. *In a Blaze of Glory: Womanist Spirituality as Social Witness*. Nashville: Abingdon Press, 1995.

———. *Womanist Justice, Womanist Hope*. Atlanta: Scholars Press, 1993.

———, ed. *A Troubling in My Soul: Womanist Perspectives on Evil and Suffering*. Maryknoll, N.Y.: Orbis Books, 1994.

Turnage, Sheila. "Saving the Dead." *American Legacy* (fall 1998): 59–64.

Vanzant, Iyanla. *The Value in the Valley: A Black Woman's Guide through Life's Dilemmas*. New York: Simon and Schuster, 1995.

Walker, Alice. *In Search of Our Mothers' Gardens*. San Diego: Harcourt Brace Jovanovich, 1983.

Walker, David. *An Appeal to the Coloured Citizens of the World*. New York: Hill and Wang, 1965.

Wallace, Michele. *Black Macho and the Myth of the Superwoman*. Reprint. New York: Warner Books, 1980.

———. "Variations on Negation and the Heresy of Black Feminist Creativity." In *Reading Black, Reading Feminist: A Critical Anthology*, edited by Henry Louis Gates Jr., 52–67. New York: Meridian Books, 1990.

Weems, Renita. *I Asked for Intimacy: Stories of Blessings, Betrayals, and Birthings*. San Diego: LuraMedia Press, 1993.

———. *Just a Sister Away: A Womanist Vision of Women's Relationships in the Bible*. San Diego: LuraMedia Press, 1988.

West, Cornel. Afterword to *The House That Race Built: Black Americans, U.S. Terrain*, edited by Wahneema Lubiano, 301–3. New York: Pantheon Books, 1997.

White, Evelyn. *Chain, Chain, Change: For Black Women Dealing with Physical and Emotional Abuse*. Seattle: Seal Press, 1985.

Williams, Delores S. "Afrocentrism and Male-Female Relationships in Church and Society." In *Living the Intersection: Womanism and Afrocentrism in Theology*, edited by Cheryl Sanders, 43–56. Minneapolis: Fortress Press, 1995.

———. "The Color of Feminism: Or Speaking the Black Woman's Tongue." *Journal of Religious Thought* 43 (1986): 42–54.

———. *Sisters in the Wilderness: The Challenge of Womanist God-Talk*. Maryknoll, N.Y.: Orbis Books, 1993.

———. "Straight Talk, Plain Talk: Womanist Words about Salvation in a Social Context." In *Embracing the Spirit: Womanist Perspectives on Hope, Salvation, and Transformation*, edited by Emilie M. Townes, 97–121. Maryknoll, N.Y.: Orbis Books, 1997.

———. "A Womanist Perspective on Sin." In *Troubling in My Soul: Womanist Perspectives on Evil and Suffering*, edited by Emilie M. Townes, 130–49. Maryknoll, N.Y.: Orbis Books, 1993.

———. "Womanist Theology: Black Women's Voices." In *Weaving the Visions: New Patterns in Feminist Spirituality*, edited by Judith Plaskow and Carol P. Christ, 179–86. San Francisco: Harper Collins, 1989.

Williams, Patricia J. *The Alchemy of Race and Rights: Diary of a Law Professor*. Cambridge, Mass.: Harvard University Press, 1991.

Willis, Susan. *Specifying: Black Women Writing the American Experience*. Madison: University of Wisconsin Press, 1987.

Wilmore, Gayraud S. *Black Religion and Black Radicalism: An Interpretation of the Religious History of Afro-American People*. 2d ed. Maryknoll, N.Y.: Orbis Books, 1998.

———, ed. *African American Religious Studies: An Interdisciplinary Theology*. Durham, N.C.: Duke University Press, 1992.

Wilson, Melba. *Crossing the Boundary: Black Women Survive Incest*. Seattle: Seal Press, 1994.

Wimbush, Vincent L. "Reading Scriptures, Reading Darkness." In *African Americans and the Bible: Sacred Texts and Social Textures*, edited by Vincent L. Wimbush, 1–43. New York: Continuum, 2001.

———, ed. *African Americans and the Bible: Sacred Texts and Social Textures*. New York: Continuum, 2001.

Young, Josiah. *A Pan-African Theology*. Trenton, N.J.: Africa World Press, 1992.

Index

activism, 112, 130–31
Africa
    cognitive orientation derived
        from, 42–44, 54, 127–28
    religions of, 132–38
    theology in, 40
    thought tradition of, 35–36,
        42–44
    women of, 103–4
*African American Special Days:
    15 Complete Worship
    Services* (Kirk-Duggan),
    126–27
African Burial Ground, New
    York City, 134
Afrocentricity, 93–96
agency, 20–21, 108–9
Akan, the, 103
Ali, Carroll Watkins, 126
Ali, Sharazad, 11
American Academy of Religion,
    56–57
anthropology
    Christian, 122
    cultural, 133, 140–43
Apostles' Creed, 114–15
*Appeal to the Colored Citizens of
    the World...* (Walker), 28
art, womanist, 140–43
Asante, Molefi, 93–96
audiation, 79
Awake, Arise, and Act (Riggs), 75

Baker-Fletcher, Garth Kasimu,
    40–41
Baker-Fletcher, Karen, 118–21,
    121–22, 129, 136
*Begrimed and Black: Christian
    Traditions on Blacks and
    Blackness* (Hood), 27
biblical scholarship, 117–18
*Black Feminist Thought: Knowl-
    edge, Consciousness, and the
    Politics of Empowerment*
    (Collins), 18, 72
*Black Macho and the Myth of the
    Superwoman* (Wallace), 29
Black Power Movement, 93–94,
    97
black theology, 5, 25, 32, 39–41,
    69, 96–98
Black Theology and Black Power
    (Cone), 25, 40–41
Black Womanist Ethics (Cannon),
    4, 68–69
*Black Women in American
    History* (Hine), 73
*Blackman's Guide to Under-
    standing the Black Woman*
    (Ali), 11
blackness in Christian tradition,
    27, 35–37
body
    black female, 13–14, 82–83,
        110
    vs. soul, 35–37

Boyd, Marsha Foster, 125–26
Brown, Teresa Fry, 124–25
Brown v. Board of Education, 3

Candomblé religion, 136, 140
Cannon, Katie G., 4, 56–57,
    59–61, 63, 68–69, 74, 76,
    79–81, 92, 100, 102
Caribbean theology, 39–40
Catholicism, 131–32
christology, 71–72, 105, 113–17
churches
    authority in, 33–34
    black, 127–32, 134
    class markers in, 17–18
    and communal life, 54
    and faith, 120
    and gender roles, 8–9, 126–29
    pastoral practices in, 62–63,
        125–29
    sexism in, 99–100, 109
churchwomen's movements,
    50–51
City of Women, The (Landes),
    140
Civil Rights Movement, 112–13,
    130–31
Clark, Septima, 113
class, social, 15–18
club women's movement, 75, 88
Collins, Patricia Hill, 18, 72, 74,
    89–90
Color Purple, The (Walker), 142
communal/community life, 54,
    63, 111–13, 119, 127–28
Cone, James H., 25, 40–41, 67,
    97–98
construction, 25–26
Cooper, Anna Julia, 121–22

Copeland, M. Shawn, 107–8
culture, 41–45, 141–43

"Decade of Women," 103
Denard, Carolyn, 134
denominations, 127–30
Detroit Metropolitan Black
    Women's Health Project,
    52–53, 57, 83
dialogue, 86–104, 129–32
Diaspora, African, 86, 102–4,
    132–38, 142
doctrine, Christian, 62, 84,
    114–15, 127
domestic labor, 7, 14
Douglas, Kelly Brown, 101–2,
    114–15, 138–39

ecclesiology, 127–29
Ecumenical Association of
    Third World Theologians
    (EATWOT), 103
ecumenical dialogue, 129–32
enslavement
    and African cognitive
        orientation, 42–44
    and Christianity, 27–31
    and gender roles, 7–8, 22
    God and, 120
    oral histories of, 59–60, 110,
        119, 134–35
    and womanist theology, 69
Erskine, Noel Leo, 39–40
ethics, 3, 58–60, 63, 76–77,
    79–81, 134–35
ethnography, 133, 140–43
Eugene, Toinette M., 52, 56,
    67–68, 138
Eurocentrism, 94–95

experiences, black women's, 71–72, 82, 84, 87, 113
Ezekiel, vision of, 102

faith, 49, 120
feminism
    black women's, 55–57, 71–74, 87–91
    white, 6, 56, 71, 89, 91–93, 95
feminist theology, 5
Fighting Words: Black Women and the Search for Justice (Collins), 18, 74

Gebara, Ivone, 38–39
Gilkes, Cheryl Townsend, 3–4, 13–14, 54, 68, 100, 142
"gender entrapment," 7, 11
gender roles, 5–12, 19–23, 29, 31–32
God
    black women and, 46, 48, 83, 99, 105, 123, 139
    different views of, 143–44
    questions about, 118–21, 123
gospel, blues, and spirituals, 108, 110, 142
Greco-Roman philosophical tradition, 35–37
Grant, Jacquelyn, 4, 68, 71–74, 105–7, 110, 112–14
Gutiérrez, Gustavo, 25

Hagar (biblical figure), 70, 82–83, 117
Hayes, Diana L., 119, 121–23, 131–32
Higginbotham, Evelyn Brooks, 12–13, 130

Hine, Darlene Clark, 49–50, 73
Hispanic theology, 38–39
historiography, emancipatory, 79–80
Holy Ghost, 120
Hood, Robert E., 27
hooks, bell, 9–10, 90
Hopkins, Dwight N., 98
Hurston, Zora Neale, 69, 81, 133, 140

In a Blaze of Glory: Womanist Spirituality as Social Witness (Townes), 75–76
In Search of Our Mothers' Gardens (Walker), 55
Islam, 28, 132

James, Joy, 90–91
jazz as a model, 46, 78–79, 81
Jesus
    as co-sufferer, 114–17
    as liberated by black women, 113–14
    ministerial vision of, 111, 115–16, 122
Jim Crow system, 69
Jones, Alice Eley, 133
Just a Sister Away (Weems), 4, 70, 82

Kalof, Linda, 11–12
Katie's Canon: Womanism and the Soul of the Black Community (Cannon), 76
King, Martin Luther, Jr., 69
kinship, 50
Kirk-Duggan, Cheryl, 118, 120, 126–27, 142

"lady" role, 5–12, 14
Landes, Ruth, 140
leadership of women, 126–29
liberation theology, 25–26, 32,
    37–42
literature of womanist theology,
    67–76
lives, contexts of, 6–7, 54–60,
    65, 76
lynching, 8

Martin, Joan M., 80–81, 134–35
McCrary, Carolyn, 136–37
men, black
    and Afrocentrism, 94–95
    and non-black women, 11
    and strong women, 29
    as theologians, 62–63, 114
methodologies, 44, 77–81
ministry
    as collaborative, 125–26
    theology and, 125–29
    women in, 100, 127–28
Mintz, Sidney, 42–43
modernity, 26–27, 33–34
Montesquieu, Charles-Louis, 27
*More Than Chains or Toil: A
    Christian Work Ethic of
    Enslaved Women* (Martin),
    80–81
motherhood, 16, 50–52, 137
Moynihan Report, 29
Mubashshir, Debra Washington,
    132
Murrell, Jeannette and Jasmine,
    142–43

Nation of Islam, 28
National Coalition for Repara-
    tions for Black Americans, 22

National Committee of Negro
    Churchmen, 97
Nicene Creed, 114–15
North Atlantic theologies, 25–27,
    35–37, 78
Ntu philosophy, 136–37

obedience, 11
ordinary theologies, 46–49, 52,
    63, 76
"othering," 34, 36
"othermothers," 51

Pan-African theology, 40–41
Pan-Africanism, 132
Parker, Ann, 59–60
participant observer, 141
pastoral
    practices, 62–63, 125–29
    theology, 124–29
Pedraja, Luis G., 38
personhood, 121–23
Phelps, Jamie, 120
political alliances, 61–62
postmodernism, 34
prayer, interactive, 48
Price, Richard, 42–43

quality-of-life tradition, 83
"Queen" role, 55, 59–60, 95

race
    construction of, 12–15
    with gender and class, 19–22
    and modernity, 34
    shifting categories of, 132
racism, 26–28, 35–37, 41, 48,
    56, 71, 95–96
rape, 8
"reading signs," 48–49

religious traditions, black, 98–
    100, 110, 119, 130, 135–38
reparations, 22
responsibility, social, 111–13
Riggs, Martha, 44–45, 74–75
Richie, Beth, 6–7

sacred space, creation of, 52–53
salvation, 106–13
Sanctified Church, The (Hurston),
    140
Schüssler Fiorenza, Elisabeth, 92
self
    in community, 112
    sense of, 6–7, 58
self-empowerment, 53
self-hatred, 21, 28
self-sacrifice, 9–10
servanthood, 110–11
sexuality, 5, 10–12, 29, 36, 55,
    110, 138–40
Shrines of the Black Madonna,
    28, 137
sin, 36–37, 109–11
single mothers
*Sisters in the Wilderness: The
    Challenge of Womanist God-
    Talk* (Williams), 60–61,
    81–85
*Sisters of the Yam: Black Women
    and Self-Recovery* (hooks),
    9–10
Sisters Working Encourag-
    ing Empowering Together
    (S.W.E.E.T.), 125
slavery. *See* enslavement
Smith, Yolanda Y., 126
"Southern belle" role, 7–8
spirituality, heritage of, 46–48,
    75–76, 133, 135–38

Stampp, Kenneth, 30
Steinberg, Martha Jean "the
    Queen," 55
stereotypes, 10–11, 14–16, 23,
    29, 49, 75–76, 138–39
suffering, 75, 106–17
survival skills, 83
syncretism, 135

teaching role, 101–2
Terrell, JoAnne Marie, 23–24,
    116–17
theology
    construction of, 25–26
    and culture, 41–45, 141–43
    dynamics of, 30–34
    ethics and, 3, 58–60
    and gender, 31–32
    and liberation, 37–42
    and ministry, 125–29
    and racism, 35–37.
    womanist, 46–64
Thomas, Linda E., 141–43
Thurman, Howard, 54, 69, 136
Tillman, Janice M., 20
Townes, Emilie, 37, 74–76, 81,
    129
Trinity, the, 118–21
*Troubling in My Soul, A: Wom-
    anist Perspectives on Evil
    and Suffering* (Townes), 75,
    81
Tubman, Harriet, 112

Unheard Voices project (Murrell),
    142–43

Vanzant, Iyanla, 137
violence, 120, 138–39
voodoo, 36, 61

Index

Wade, Bruce, 11–12

Walker, Alice, 13–14, 55–57, 68,
    89–90, 138

Walker, David, 28

Wallace, Michele, 19, 29

Watson, Jo Anne, 22, 99

Weems, Renita, 4, 68–71, 74, 81,
    82, 117–18

Wells Barnett, Ida, 74–75,
    112

*White Women's Christ, Black
    Women's Jesus* (Grant), 4,
    71, 106–7

"Who Am I?" (Tillman), 20

Williams, Delores S., 4, 21–22,
    60–62, 67–68, 81–85, 95,
    97, 110–13, 115–17

Williams, Patricia, 12–13

Wimbush, Vincent L., 118

Winfrey, Oprah, 19, 70

"woman" category, 92

*Womanist Justice, Womanist
    Hope* (Townes), 74–75

womanist theology
    and academy, 32
    and black theology, 96–98
    development of, 46–64
    dialogue and, 86–104
    and ethics, 58–60, 76–77, 90
    and ethnography, 140–43
    as experientially based, 71–72,
        82, 84, 87
    vs. feminism, 88–93
    jazz and, 46, 78–79, 81
    key points in, 63–64
    literature of, 67–76
    methodologies for, 77–81
    teaching of, 101–2
    Walker's definition and, 13–
        14, 55–57, 63, 68, 89–90,
        138–39

WomanistCare, 125–26

work, 14–16

World Council of Churches, 103

Young, Josiah, 40–41

Yoruba religion, 137

Of Related Interest

If It Wasn't for the Women
Cheryl Townsend Gilkes
ISBN 1-57075-343-1

One of the foremost womanist scholars of religion
explores the complex interrelation of gender, race, and
class that makes up the experience of black women.

"*If It Wasn't for the Women* is an indispensable read for
anyone wanting to learn about the vibrant faith and life
of black women, who continue to struggle for justice and
dignity within both the church and the wider society."
— *The Other Side*

Introducing Black Theology
Dwight N. Hopkins
ISBN 1-57075-286-9

"An essential introduction to a theology rooted in
the religious experience of African Americans in slavery,
refined through generations of struggle and hope,
and articulated in the past thirty years by
two generations of scholars."
— James H. Cone,
Union Theological Seminary

Please support your local bookstore, or call 1-800-258-5838.

For a free catalog, please write us at
Orbis Books, Box 302
Maryknoll, NY 10545-0302
or visit our website at www.orbisbooks.com

Thank you for reading *Introducing Womanist Theology*.
We hope you enjoyed it.